Just Enough for Two

or one

Cookbook

By Sharon McFall and Linda Burgett
with Shelley Plettl

CREATIVE IDEAS

First Printing 2006

3,500 copies

ISBN: 1-930170-20-3

Additional copies may be ordered for $18.95/each, plus $3.50 shipping.

Creative Ideas Publishing
7916 N.W. 23rd Street
P.M.B. 115
Bethany, OK 73008-5135

Order by phone: 800/673-0786
Or on the web: www.busywomanscookbook.com

CONTENTS

ABOUT THE AUTHORS

JUST ENOUGH FOR TWO is coauthored by Sharon McFall and her two daughters, Linda Burgett and Shelley Plettl.

SHARON MCFALL is a native of Des Moines, Iowa, and has worked extensively in publicity and promotion and in the retail management field. She gained her knowledge of cooking and food as the mother of four children with diverse tastes, and as an executive with a dinner theatre. She and her husband have owned and operated a restaurant and concessions in tourist areas. Sharon is the coauthor of six cookbooks, including the national best seller, BUSY WOMAN'S COOKBOOK, which has sold over half a million copies.

LINDA BURGETT lives in New Mexico with her husband, Stan, and son Tyler. Her love of different cultures and cuisine makes traveling around the United States and the world as Executive Producer of Passion Play Ministries a true pleasure. She enjoys entertaining and collecting recipes at the many functions she attends. She is the author of the highly successful MILD TO WILD MEXICAN COOKBOOK, and was coauthor with her mother of BUSY WOMAN'S SLOW COOKER COOKBOOK.

SHELLEY PLETTL has plenty of experience in the kitchen-trying to satisfy the appetites of three very active daughters and a husband who is a speed, strength and conditioning coach for professional athletes. Her love of food and cooking led her into the restaurant business in the Ozarks resort town of Eureka Springs, Arkansas, and the country music center, Renfro Valley, Kentucky. She now resides in Tallahassee, Florida. Shelley is the author of the very popular IF I GOTTA COOK MAKE IT QUICK COOKBOOK.

FOREWORD

Our society today has many people living as couples or as individuals: retired couples whose families are on their own, couples who have never had children, students, and both men and women living alone by choice or by necessity.

Most cookbooks are designed for families of four or more. As we have traveled all around the United States with our cookbooks, common statements are: "It's just the two of us." "I live alone." "If I bought a cookbook it would be just to read. I would never use it because the recipes make too much."

We felt that there was a need for a cookbook with delicious recipes for one or two people. Not only are the ingredients cut down, but JUST ENOUGH FOR TWO features quick and easy recipes with only a few ingredients—a cookbook that couples and singles can and will use over and over.

It is an everyday cookbook for daily use by the young, the mature, or the senior cook.

NOTES

_____
_____
_____
_____
_____
_____
_____
_____
_____
_____
_____
_____
_____
_____
_____
_____
_____
_____
_____
_____
_____
_____
_____
_____
_____
_____
_____
_____
_____
_____
_____
_____
_____
_____
_____
_____

Beverages & Appetizers

DRINK YOUR FRUIT SMOOTHIE

1 cup pineapple juice
1 cup pineapple tidbits
¾ cup fresh or frozen raspberries
1 small banana, sliced
2 teaspoons sugar
2 ice cubes

In blender, combine all ingredients. Cover. Blend until smooth. Serve in tall glasses.

CHOCOLATY SMOOTHIES

1 cup vanilla yogurt
¾ cup milk
1 small ripe banana, frozen, cut into chunks
3 tablespoons chocolate drink mix
⅛ teaspoon vanilla

In blender, combine all ingredients. Cover. Blend until smooth.

EARLY MORNING SMOOTHIES

1½ cups sliced strawberries
½ cup vanilla yogurt
½ cup milk
1 tablespoon dry milk powder
1 tablespoon sugar
1 tablespoon strawberry jam

In blender, combine all ingredients. Cover. Blend until smooth.

SNACK-IN-A-GLASS

⅓ cup milk
3 tablespoons chocolate syrup
1 pint vanilla ice cream
1 small banana

In blender, combine all ingredients. Cover. Blend until smooth.

ELVIS SMOOTHIE

2 bananas, sliced
2 tablespoons creamy peanut butter
2 scoops frozen vanilla yogurt
½ cup milk

In blender, combine all ingredients. Cover. Blend until smooth.

BLUEBERRY SMOOTHIE

1 cup frozen blueberries
¾ cup milk
¼ cup frozen orange juice concentrate
⅛ teaspoon cinnamon
4 ice cubes

In blender, combine all ingredients. Cover. Blend until smooth.

DOUBLE FRUIT SMOOTHIE

> 2 cups frozen sliced peaches
> ½ cup frozen strawberries
> ⅓ cup chilled cranberry juice
> 2 tablespoons sugar

In blender, combine all ingredients. Cover. Blend until smooth. Pour into 2 glasses.

STRAWBERRY SMOOTHIE

> 2 (4 ounce) containers strawberry
> flavored yogurt
> 1 cup frozen strawberries
> ¼ cup milk

In blender, combine all ingredients. Cover. Blend until smooth.

PINK PEACH SHAKE

> 1 cup milk
> ½ of (6 ounce) can frozen pink lemonade
> 1 (12 ounce) package frozen peaches,
> slightly thawed
> 1 pint vanilla ice cream

In blender, combine all ingredients, except ice cream. Cover. Blend until smooth. Add ice cream. Cover. Blend until just smooth.

ORANGE VANILLA SHAKE

1 (6 ounce) can frozen orange juice
1 cup vanilla ice cream
½ cup milk

In blender, combine all ingredients. Cover. Blend until smooth.

CHOCO-NUTTY SHAKE

1 cup cold milk
2 tablespoons chocolate syrup
2 tablespoons peanut butter
1 pint vanilla ice cream, softened

In blender, combine all ingredients, except ice cream. Cover. Blend until smooth. Add ice cream. Cover. Blend until smooth.

CHOCOLATE BANANA SHAKE

2 bananas, sliced
1⅓ cups milk
1 cup chocolate ice cream
⅓ cup chocolate syrup

In blender, combine all ingredients. Cover. Blend until smooth.

STEPHEN J. POPLAWSKI INVENTED
THE BLENDER IN 1922.

BANANA CREAM SHAKE

2 cups vanilla ice cream
1 banana
½ cup half-and-half

In blender, combine all ingredients. Cover. Blend until smooth.

STRAWBERRY SODA

1 cup milk
½ cup vanilla ice cream, softened
½ cup sliced strawberries
2 tablespoons sugar
1 cup ginger ale, chilled

In blender, combine milk, ice cream, strawberries, and sugar. Cover. Blend until smooth. Pour into 2 tall glasses. Add ginger ale.

OLD FASHIONED CHOCOLATE SODA

½ cup chocolate syrup
1 cup carbonated water
2 scoops vanilla ice cream

In two tall glasses, add to each ¼ cup syrup and ½ cup water. Mix well. Add ice cream

AFRICAN-AMERICAN INVENTOR
J. THOMAS WHITE DEVISED THE LEMON
SQUEEZER IN 1896.

FROSTY ORANGE DRINK

½ cup milk
½ cup cold water
⅓ cup frozen orange juice
½ teaspoon vanilla
¼ cup sugar
6 ice cubes

In blender, combine all ingredients. Cover. Blend until smooth.

FRUIT PUNCH

1 (12 ounce) can lemon-lime soda, chilled
1 cup cranberry juice, chilled
½ cup pineapple juice, chilled
¼ cup orange juice, chilled

In pitcher, combine all ingredients. Mix well. Serve over ice.

LEISURELY AFTERNOON PUNCH

2 cups cold water
¼ cup sweetened lemonade drink mix
⅓ cup cranberry juice
¾ cup lemon lime soda

In pitcher, combine all ingredients. Mix well. Serve in tall glasses with ice.

MARSHMALLOW HOT CHOCOLATE

2 cups milk

¾ cup miniature marshmallows

2 teaspoons baking cocoa

2 teaspoons sugar

½ teaspoon vanilla

In small saucepan, combine milk, marshmallows, cocoa, and sugar. Over medium heat cook until marshmallows are melted. Remove from heat, stir in vanilla.

HOT CHOCOLATE TOFFEE

2 cups milk

¼ cup water

¼ cup sugar

3 ounces dark chocolate, chopped

¼ cup butterscotch chips

In small saucepan, combine all ingredients. Over low heat cook until hot. Mix well. Serve warm. Garnish with whipped topping and crushed toffee bar if desired.

ON CHILLY NIGHTS MOCHA

2 cups strong coffee

⅔ cup sweetened condensed milk

1 (1 ounce) square unsweetened chocolate

¼ teaspoon cinnamon

Whipped cream

In medium saucepan, combine all ingredients, except whipped cream. Mix well. Over medium heat cook until hot. Serve in mugs. Top with whipped cream.

CARAMEL COFFEE

2 mugs of hot coffee
4 tablespoons caramel ice cream topping
2 tablespoons whipped cream

In each mug, add 2 tablespoons caramel topping, mix well. Top with whipped cream.

JUMP START COFFEE

1 cup half-and-half
1 cup strong coffee
6 tablespoons maple syrup

In small saucepan, combine all ingredients. Mix well. Over medium heat cook until hot.

MOCHA LATTE

2 cups hot coffee,
4 tablespoons half-and-half
2 tablespoons chocolate syrup
2 teaspoons sugar
2 tablespoons whipped topping

In 2 mugs, add to each, 1 cup coffee, 2 tablespoons half-and-half, 1 tablespoon chocolate, and 1 teaspoon sugar. Mix well. Top each with whipped topping.

ICED COFFEE

> 2 cups milk
>
> 2 tablespoons chocolate syrup
>
> 2 teaspoons instant espresso-coffee powder
>
> 4 ice cubes
>
> ¼ teaspoon cinnamon

In blender, combine all ingredients, except cinnamon. Cover. Blend. Pour into 2 glasses. Sprinkle cinnamon on top.

TWO CUPS OF HOT CIDER

> 2 cups apple cider
>
> 2½ teaspoons orange flavored breakfast drink powder
>
> ⅛ teaspoon cinnamon

In small saucepan, combine all ingredients. Over medium heat cook until hot.

SPICY HOT CIDER

> 2 cups apple cider
>
> ¼ cup red cinnamon candies

In small saucepan, combine all ingredients. Over medium heat stir until candies melt and cider is hot.

BLOOMING ONION

2 cups flour

1¾ cups beer

½ teaspoon Cajun seasoning

1 onion

Peanut oil for frying

In medium bowl, combine flour, beer, and Cajun seasoning. Mix well. Set aside for 3 hours. Cut onion stem up, starting ½ inch from stem, slice ½-inch thick sections keeping them attached to the stem. Place onion in beer batter stem side down. Spoon batter over onion, covering all slices and spreading slightly to separate the slices. Place in 350 degree oil until golden brown. Remove, drain. Serve with Ranch or Thousand Island dressing.

DEEP FRIED MUSHROOMS

½ cup complete pancake mix

¼ cup water

Oil for frying

10 white mushrooms

In small bowl, combine pancake mix and water. Mix well. In medium skillet, add oil to 2 inches, heat over high heat. Dip mushrooms in pancake mix, drop into hot oil. Fry until golden brown. Serve with Ranch dressing.

TO KEEP POPCORN, POTATO CHIPS AND OTHER MUNCHIES FRESH, STORE THEM IN THE FREEZER UNTIL READY TO EAT.

GOLDEN FRIED CHEESE

Cheddar or Swiss cheese, cut in ½-inch cubes
2 eggs, beaten
½ cup bread crumbs
Oil

Dip cheese cubes in eggs then roll in bread crumbs. Spear cheese cubes, place in deep fat fryer. Cook until golden brown.

CRUNCHY VEGETABLE

1 egg, beaten
1 cup broccoli florets
1 cup cauliflower florets
1 cup finely crushed seasoned bread crumbs

Preheat oven to 425 degrees. Dip vegetables in egg, roll in crumbs. Place on greased baking sheet. Bake 20 minutes or until golden brown. Serve with Ranch dressing.

PEPPERONI PITA PIZZA

1 (6 inch) pita bread
¼ cup diced pepperoni
¼ cup shredded mozzarella cheese

Preheat oven to 350 degrees. Place pita on baking sheet. Sprinkle pepperoni on pita. Top with cheese. Bake 10 minutes or until cheese is melted. Cut into wedges. Serve warm.

CRAB MUFFINS

2 English muffins, split

½ cup diced imitation crab meat

⅓ cup cheese sauce

2 tablespoons butter or margarine, softened

¼ teaspoon garlic salt

Preheat oven to 350 degrees. Place muffins on baking sheet. In small bowl, combine remaining ingredients. Mix well. Spread mixture on muffins. Bake 10 minutes or until golden brown. Cut into wedges. Serve warm.

CRAB SPREAD

1 (3 ounce) package cream cheese with onion, softened

¼ cup mayonnaise

1 tablespoon ketchup

1 (6 ounce) can crabmeat, drained, flaked

In small bowl, combine cream cheese, mayonnaise, and ketchup. Mix well. Fold in crabmeat. Mix well. Serve with crackers.

ADD ONE TEASPOON OF SALT TO COLD WATER BEFORE BOILING EGGS TO MAKE THEM EASIER TO PEEL.

CHILLED CRAB DIP

½ cup chopped cooked crab
2 tablespoons chopped scallions
¾ cup sour cream
½ tablespoon creamy horseradish

In small bowl, combine all ingredients. Mix well. Cover. Chill.

SEAFOOD DIP

1 (8 ounce) package cream cheese, softened
½ cup chopped cooked shrimp
⅓ cup chopped imitation crab meat
1 cup shrimp cocktail sauce

In medium bowl, combine cream cheese, shrimp, crab, and ½ cup shrimp cocktail sauce. Mix well. Add mixture to small bowl. Spread remaining cocktail sauce over top. Serve with crackers.

SALSA DIP

¼ cup salsa
½ cup sour cream

In small bowl, combine ingredients. Mix well.

SALSA RANCH DIP

⅓ cup chunky salsa
¼ cup Ranch dressing

In small bowl, combine ingredients. Mix well. Serve with breadsticks or chips.

ONION AND SOUR CREAM DUNK

¼ cup sour cream
¼ cup Miracle Whip®
¼ cup cheese spread
1 teaspoon dry onion soup mix

In small bowl, combine all ingredients. Beat until smooth. Chill until ready to serve. Serve with vegetable dippers or chips.

ONION DIP

1 cup finely chopped onion
½ tablespoon butter or margarine
½ teaspoon paprika
½ cup sour cream

In small skillet, sauté onion in butter, over medium high heat until tender. Stir in paprika. Mix well. In small bowl, combine all ingredients. Mix well.

TWO CHEESE VEGGIE DIP

1 (8 ounce) container vegetable cream cheese
½ cup cottage cheese
2 tablespoons water
½ teaspoon garlic salt

In blender, combine all ingredients. Cover. Blend until well mixed. Serve with fresh vegetables, chips or crackers.

SIMPLE CREAM CHEESE DIP

¼ cup cream cheese

¼ cup mayonnaise

2 tablespoons diced onion

1 tablespoon milk

In small bowl, combine all ingredients. Mix well.

ALFREDO & PASTA DIP

½ cup Alfredo sauce

½ cup pasta sauce

½ cup shredded mozzarella cheese

¼ cup diced pepperoni

In small saucepan, combine all ingredients. Mix well. Over low heat cook 10 minutes. Serve with bread sticks.

HONEY MUSTARD DIP

½ cup honey

¼ cup Dijon mustard

In small bowl, combine honey and mustard. Mix well. Serve with chicken fingers or fresh vegetables.

HONEY OF A FRUIT DIP

1 cup vanilla yogurt

1 teaspoon honey

¼ teaspoon almond extract

In small bowl, combine all ingredients. Mix well. Serve with mixed fruit.

DIP AND EAT FRESH FRUIT DIP

½ cup whipped topping

½ cup strawberry yogurt

¼ cup diced strawberries

In small bowl, combine all ingredients. Mix well. Serve with fresh fruit.

ASSORTMENT OF FRUIT DIP

1 (4 ounce) package cream cheese

1 cup Cool Whip®

½ cup orange juice

In blender, combine all ingredients. Cover. Blend until smooth. Chill. Serve with assortment of fruit.

FRUIT DIP

1 (8 ounce) container cream cheese, softened

⅓ cup brown sugar

2 tablespoons milk

½ teaspoon vanilla

In small bowl, combine all ingredients. Mix well. Serve with fruit.

TO KEEP SLICED APPLES FROM TURNING BROWN, KEEP THEM IN A BOWL OF WATER WITH A TABLESPOON OF LEMON JUICE.

CARAMEL DIP

13 caramel candies
2 tablespoons milk
1 tablespoon peanut butter

In medium microwave bowl, combine all ingredients. Microwave on high 2 to 3 minutes or until melted. Stir after each minute. Serve with apple and banana slices or vanilla wafer cookies.

PARMESAN CHIPS

½ cup shredded Parmesan cheese (not grated)

Preheat oven to 375 degrees. Drop cheese by tablespoon, onto nonstick cookie sheet, spread cheese to form 2-inch circle, 3 inches apart. Bake 5 to 7 minutes or until edges begin to slightly brown. Don't over cook. Cool before removing from sheet.

GUACAMOLE

1 large avocado, peeled, pit removed
1 tablespoon salsa
½ tablespoon sour cream
¼ teaspoon onion salt

In small bowl, mash avocado. Add remaining ingredients. Mix well. Serve with tortilla chips.

PEANUT BUTTER & JELLY TORTILLA

½ tablespoon cream cheese

½ teaspoon peanut butter

1 (6-inch) flour tortilla

½ teaspoon grape jelly

In small bowl, combine cream cheese and peanut butter. Mix well. Spread peanut butter mixture over tortilla. Spread jelly over peanut butter. Roll up tortilla; slice into 1-inch pieces.

MARINATED OLIVES

1 tablespoon red wine vinegar

1 tablespoon olive oil

½ teaspoon pepper

½ cup green olives, drained

½ cup black olives, drained

In small bowl, combine vinegar, oil, and pepper. Mix well. Add olives, toss to coat. Refrigerate at least 30 minutes.

OUT ON TRAIL MIX

1 cup Golden Grahams® cereal

¼ cup M&M's® candy

¼ cup raisins

¼ cup dried banana chips

¼ cup dry roasted peanuts

In medium bowl, combine all ingredients. Mix well.

HONEY BEAR CRUNCH

2 cups corn cereal squares

¾ cup miniature pretzels

½ cup pecan halves

2 tablespoons plus 2 teaspoons
butter or margarine

2 tablespoons honey

Preheat oven to 350 degrees. In 9 x 9-inch baking pan, combine cereal, pretzels, and pecans. In small bowl, combine butter and honey. Mix well. Drizzle over cereal mixture. Mix well. Bake 12 to 15 minutes, stirring occasionally. Spread on wax paper to cool.

HOT ROASTED PEANUTS

½ pound raw peanuts

1½ teaspoons peanut oil

½ teaspoon salt

Preheat oven to 350 degrees. In medium bowl, combine all ingredients. Mix well. Spread in baking pan. Bake 20 to 30 minutes or until lightly brown.

HOLIDAY CANDIED WALNUTS

1 egg white

1 (6 ounce) package walnut halves

¾ cup sugar

1 teaspoon ground cinnamon

Preheat oven to 300 degrees. In medium bowl, beat egg white until frothy. Add walnuts, toss to coat. In shallow bowl, combine sugar and cinnamon. Mix well. Place nuts in mixture, toss to coat. Place nuts on cookie sheet coated with cooking spray. Bake 15 minutes. Stir. Bake 20 minutes. Let cool. Break apart any clusters.

DEVILED EGGS

2 hard cooked eggs
1 tablespoon Miracle Whip® salad dressing
Dash of mustard
¼ teaspoon sugar

Cut eggs in halves. Slip out yolks, mash with fork. Add remaining ingredients. Mix well. Sprinkle with paprika (optional). Chill.

PIZZA MUNCHIES NACHOS

½ cup ground beef
1 cup pasta sauce
¼ cup chopped pepperoni
1 (8½ ounce) bag tortilla chips
1 cup shredded mozzarella

In medium skillet, brown ground beef over medium heat. Drain. Add pasta sauce and pepperoni. Over low heat, cook 5 minutes or until hot. Arrange tortilla chips over serving platter. Top with meat mixture. Sprinkle with cheese.

BUFFALO CHICKEN WINGS

⅓ cup hot sauce

2 tablespoons butter or margarine, melted

⅛ teaspoon cayenne pepper

⅛ teaspoon black pepper

1 pound chicken wings, separated, tips discarded

Preheat grill. In small bowl, combine all ingredients, except chicken. Mix well. Coat chicken with sauce. Grill 10 to 12 minutes on each side, brushing with sauce during cooking. Serve with ranch dressing.

SWEET AND SAVORY CHICKEN WINGS

½ cup French salad dressing

¼ cup dark corn syrup

½ tablespoon Worcestershire sauce

2 teaspoons from French onion soup mix packet

1 pound chicken wings, separated, tips discarded

Preheat oven to 400 degrees. In small bowl, combine all ingredients, except chicken. Mix well. Coat chicken with sauce, place in 13 x 9 x 2-inch baking dish. Drizzle remaining sauce over chicken. Bake 35 minutes or until fully cooked, turning during the last 5 minutes of cooking.

EASY CHICKEN WINGS

½ cup mayonnaise

1 tablespoon Tabasco® sauce

1 pound chicken wings, separated, tips discarded

Preheat oven to 400 degrees. In small bowl, combine mayonnaise and Tabasco. Mix well. Coat wings with sauce, place on baking sheet. Bake 35 minutes or until fully cooked, turning during the last 5 minutes of cooking.

PARTY COCKTAIL WIENERS

1 (16 ounce) package cocktail wieners

½ cup ketchup

½ cup barbecue sauce

½ cup packed brown sugar

½ teaspoon Worcestershire sauce

In slow cooker, combine all ingredients. Cover. Cook on high 1 hour. Remove lid. Cook on low 40 to 50 minutes.

CHILLED SHRIMP APPETIZERS

12 fresh medium shrimp in shells

1 (12 ounce) can beer

1 bay leaf

¼ teaspoon red pepper flakes

In medium saucepan, combine shrimp and beer. Over medium heat bring to a boil. Add bay leaf and red pepper. Reduce heat to low. Cover. Simmer until shrimp is bright pink, about 5 minutes. Drain. Chill. Serve with cocktail sauce.

SPECIAL PARTY GREEN BEAN BUNDLES

1 (16 ounce) package sliced bacon
3 (14½ ounce) cans whole green beans, drained
¾ cup packed brown sugar
½ cup butter
¾ teaspoon garlic powder
½ teaspoon pepper
¼ teaspoon Worcestershire sauce

Preheat oven to 350 degrees. Cut each bacon slice in half cross-wise. Lay 7 beans on 1 end of bacon slice, wrap bacon around green beans. Put bundle in 13 x 9-inch baking dish. Repeat with remaining beans and bacon. In medium saucepan, combine remaining ingredients. Mix well. Over medium heat cook until mixture is hot and butter has melted. Pour over beans. Cover. Bake 30 minutes. Uncover. Bake 15 minutes. Makes 24.

UP BEAT CARROT STICKS

2 carrots, sliced in sticks
½ cup orange juice
1 tablespoon sugar

In medium bowl, combine all ingredients. Cover. Chill 2 hours. Drain and serve.

Soups & Salads

CHICKEN & RICE SOUP

2½ cups chicken broth

1 carrot, peeled, diced

½ celery stalk, diced

1 cup diced cooked chicken

½ cup cooked rice

In large saucepan, add chicken broth, carrot, and celery. Over medium high heat bring to a boil. Reduce heat to low, simmer 15 minutes or until vegetables are tender. Add chicken and rice, cook until hot. Salt and pepper to taste.

QUICK LUNCH WITH SOUP

1 (10¾ ounce) can cream of chicken soup

½ cup broccoli florets, thawed

½ cup chopped cooked chicken

¾ cup milk

In medium saucepan, combine all ingredients. Mix well. Over medium heat cook until hot.

VEGETABLE BEEF SOUP

½ pound stew beef, browned

1½ cups tomato juice

1 cup beef broth

1 (10 ounce) package frozen mixed vegetables

In 3-quart slow cooker, combine all ingredients. Mix well. Cover. Cook on low 6 to 8 hours.

HAMBURGER VEGETABLE SOUP

½ pound ground beef, browned
1 cup beef broth
1 cup tomato juice
½ cup chopped tomatoes
1 cup frozen mixed vegetables
1 teaspoon salt

In 3-quart slow cooker, combine all ingredients. Mix well. Cover. Cook on low 5 to 6 hours.

BEEF TOMATO SOUP

½ pound ground beef, browned
1½ cups cubed potatoes
½ cup chopped onions
1 (8 ounce) can tomato sauce
½ cup tomato juice

In 1½-quart slow cooker, combine all ingredients. Mix well. Cover. Cook on low 6 to 8 hours.

POTATO SAUSAGE SOUP

2 cups vegetable juice
1 cup chili with beans
1½ cups cubed potatoes
1 smoked sausage link, sliced
1 (8 ounce) can tomato sauce

In 3-quart slow cooker, combine all ingredients. Mix well. Cover. Cook on low 6 to 8 hours.

SUPER FAST OYSTER SOUP

2 tablespoons butter

½ pint oysters, undrained

1 cup milk

½ cup cream

Salt and pepper

In medium saucepan, melt butter over low heat. Add oysters. Simmer until oysters curl. Add milk, cream, and salt and pepper to taste. Cook until hot, stirring constantly.

CLAMS & SHRIMP SOUP

1 (10¾ ounce) can clam chowder soup

½ cup chopped shrimp

½ cup milk

⅓ cup half-and-half

In medium saucepan, combine all ingredients. Mix well. Over low heat cook 10 to 15 minutes.

SHRIMP CLAM CHOWDER

1 (10¾ ounce) can clam chowder soup

½ cup corn

½ cup chopped cooked shrimp

1 cup milk

In medium saucepan, combine all ingredients. Mix well. Over low heat simmer 10 minutes.

MEXICAN BEAN SOUP

    1 (1-inch thick) pork chop, diced
    ¼ cup chopped onion
    1 cup chicken broth
    1 cup Mexican-style chopped tomatoes
    1 (15 ounce) can pinto beans, drained
    1 teaspoon chili powder

In medium saucepan, brown pork and onion over medium heat. Add remaining ingredients, bring to a boil. Reduce heat to low. Cover. Simmer 10 minutes.

OLD MEXICO BLACK BEAN SOUP

    ½ cup water
    1 (16 ounce) jar chunky salsa
    1 small onion, chopped
    ⅓ cup frozen corn
    1 cup black beans, drained
    ½ pound beef stew meat

In 3-quart slow cooker, combine all ingredients. Mix well. Cover. Cook on low 6 to 8 hours.

COWBOY BEAN SOUP

½ pound ground beef

⅓ cup chopped onions

1 (10¾ ounce) can ranch style beans

1 (4 ounce) can green chiles

⅓ cup diced tomatoes

In medium saucepan, brown beef over medium heat. Drain. Add remaining ingredients. Mix well. Reduce heat to low. Simmer 30 minutes.

SHORT-CUT BEAN SOUP

1 (15 ounce) can navy beans

2 tablespoons butter

⅓ cup chopped cooked ham

In small saucepan, combine all ingredients. Mix well. Over medium heat cook until hot.

GREEN CHILE SOUP

1 (10¾ ounce) can cheddar cheese soup

½ cup water

⅓ cup chopped tomatoes

1 (4 ounce) can diced green chiles

¼ cup chopped onions

In medium saucepan, combine all ingredients. Mix well. Cover. Over low heat cook 15 minutes.

FRENCH ONION SOUP

2 cups sliced onion

2 tablespoons butter

2 cups beef broth

2 teaspoons Worcestershire sauce

1 teaspoon salt

In medium saucepan, combine onions and butter. Over medium heat cook until lightly browned. Add remaining ingredients. Reduce heat to low. Cook 15 minutes.

BEST FOR LESS SOUP

1 (10¾ ounce) can Italian tomato soup

1 can water

1 cup cooked vegetables

1 cup cooked macaroni

½ teaspoon salt

In medium saucepan, combine all ingredients. Mix well. Over medium heat bring to a boil.

EGG DROP SOUP

1 (14½ ounce) can chicken broth

1 stalk celery, chopped

1 tablespoon chopped green onion

Dash ground ginger

Dash hot pepper sauce

1 large egg, beaten

In medium saucepan, combine all ingredients, except egg. Over medium heat bring to a boil. Slowly pour egg so it will form thin shreds.

HOMEMADE POTATO SOUP

2 medium potatoes, peeled, cubed

⅓ cup chopped onion

1 stalk celery, chopped

¼ cup shredded cheddar cheese

2½ cups milk

1 tablespoon butter or margarine

In medium saucepan, combine potatoes, onions and celery, cover with water. Over medium heat cook until tender. Drain. Add cheese, milk, butter, and salt and pepper to taste. Cook until hot.

BROCCOLI CHEESE SOUP

½ (10 ounce) package frozen chopped broccoli

1 (10¾ ounce) can cream of celery soup

1 carrot, chopped

½ cup shredded cheddar cheese

In medium saucepan, combine all ingredients. Over low heat simmer 30 to 40 minutes.

CHILL CHASER PORK STEW

1 cup sliced potatoes

½ pound pork roast, cut into 1-inch pieces

1 (12 ounce) jar chicken gravy

1 cup canned black eyed peas, rinsed, drained

In 1½-quart slow cooker, combine all ingredients. Mix well. Cover. Cook on low 5 to 6 hours.

CHILI READY IN MINUTES

½ pound ground beef, cooked, drained
1 cup diced tomatoes
1 (14 ounce) can kidney beans, undrained
¼ cup chopped onions
2 tablespoons Chili-O® seasoning mix

In medium saucepan, combine all ingredients. Over medium heat bring to a boil. Cover. Reduce heat to low. Simmer 15 minutes.

CHICKEN & RICE SALAD

1 cup halved seedless red grapes
⅔ cup diced cooked chicken
⅔ cup cooked rice
¼ cup chopped walnuts
3 tablespoons Italian dressing

In medium bowl, combine all ingredients. Mix well.

CHEESY PEA SALAD

1½ cups frozen peas, thawed
½ cup shredded cheddar cheese
¼ cup Miracle Whip®
2 tablespoons finely diced onion
¼ teaspoon mustard

In small bowl, combine all ingredients. Mix well. Cover. Chill until serving.

BERRY & PORK LOIN SALAD

        3 cups torn romaine lettuce
        ¼ cup sliced celery
        4 ounces pork tenderloin, cooked, sliced thin
        1 cup sliced strawberries
        2 tablespoons Sugared Pecans (recipe follows)
        Honey & Balsamic Dressing (recipe follows)

In bowl, layer lettuce, celery, pork, and strawberries. Sprinkle Sugared Pecans over top. Serve with Honey & Balsamic dressing.

Sugared Pecans

        ½ cup pecan halves
        ¼ cup sugar
        1 tablespoon butter

In small skillet, combine all ingredients over medium high heat. Reduce heat to low when sugar begins to melt. Cook until sugar is golden brown. Pour onto buttered baking sheet. Cool.

Honey & Balsamic Dressing

        1 clove garlic, minced
        1½ tablespoons olive oil
        2 tablespoons honey
        2 tablespoons balsamic vinegar
        2 tablespoons water

In small skillet, sauté garlic in oil, over medium heat for 30 seconds. Add remaining ingredients. Cook until heated. Cool.

STEAK SALAD

½ pound beef top round steak

2 teaspoons grill seasoning

4 cups mixed salad greens

6 cherry tomatoes, halved

Juiced Up Dressing (recipe follows)

Season steak with grill seasoning. Grill or fry steak to desired doneness. Cut into thin strips. Place greens in bowls. Top with tomatoes and steak. Serve with dressing.

Juiced Up Dressing

1 cup spicy vegetable juice

1 tablespoon olive oil

½ tablespoon red wine vinegar

¼ teaspoon garlic salt

In small bowl, combine all ingredients. Mix well. Cover. Chill at least 30 minutes before serving.

LEFTOVER TURKEY SALAD

1 cup chopped, cooked turkey

¼ cup chopped celery

¼ cup sliced red grapes

2 tablespoons chopped walnuts

⅓ cup Miracle Whip®

1 teaspoon sugar

In medium bowl, combine all ingredients. Mix well. Cover. Chill. Serve on lettuce or with bread.

SHOW OFF TUNA SALAD

2 small/medium tomatoes
½ cup cottage cheese
1 (6 ounce) can white tuna, drained
2 tablespoons diced celery

Scoop pulp from tomatoes. In small bowl, combine cottage cheese, tuna, and celery. Mix well. Spoon mixture into tomatoes. Place tomatoes on plates with lettuce leaves.

ORANGE SPINACH SALAD

4 cups spinach leaves
¼ cup Mandarin oranges
2 tablespoons sliced almonds
Orange Vinaigrette Dressing (recipe follows)

Place spinach in bowls. Top with oranges and almonds. Serve with dressing.

Orange Vinaigrette Dressing

2 tablespoons plus 2 teaspoons orange juice
1 tablespoon olive oil
½ teaspoon sugar
¼ teaspoon garlic salt

In small bowl, combine all ingredients. Mix well.

WRAPPING CELERY IN ALUMINUM FOIL BEFORE YOU REFRIGERATE IT WILL HELP IT KEEP LONGER.

HONEY MUSTARD SALAD

> 4 cups mixed salad greens
> ¼ cup halved cherry tomatoes
> ¼ cup chopped honey roasted peanuts
> Honey Mustard Dressing (recipe follows)

In 2 bowls layer salad and tomatoes. Sprinkle peanuts on top. Serve with dressing.

Honey Mustard Dressing

> 2 tablespoons honey
> 1½ tablespoons Dijon mustard
> 1½ tablespoons olive oil
> ½ tablespoon apple cider vinegar

In small bowl, combine all ingredients. Mix well.

BLUE CHEESE SALAD WEDGES

> ½ head iceberg lettuce, cut in two wedges
> ½ cup Blue Cheese Dressing (recipe follows)
> 2 slices bacon, cooked, crumbled
> 2 tablespoons blue cheese

On two plates, place wedges tip side up. Drizzle with dressing. Sprinkle bacon and cheese over top.

Blue Cheese Dressing

> ¼ cup sour cream
> 2 tablespoons crumbled blue cheese
> ¼ teaspoon Dijon mustard
> ¼ teaspoon garlic salt

In small bowl, combine all ingredients. Mix well.

BBQ CHICKEN SALAD

- 2 tablespoons barbeque sauce
- 1 tablespoon mayonnaise
- 1 boneless, skinless, chicken breast, cooked, cubed
- 2 stalks celery, chopped
- ¼ cup red onion, diced
- ½ cup canned sweet corn, drained

In medium bowl, combine all ingredients. Mix well.

EASY & QUICK TACO SALAD

- ½ pound lean ground beef
- 2 tablespoons taco seasoning
- 2 cups corn chips
- 1¼ cups shredded lettuce
- ⅓ cup chopped tomatoes
- ¼ cup chopped onions
- ¼ cup shredded cheddar cheese

In small skillet, brown beef over medium heat. Add taco seasoning and 2 tablespoons water. Cook 2 minutes. Arrange corn chips on two plates. Top with beef, lettuce, tomatoes, onions, and cheese.

TO EXTEND THE LIFE OF FRESH PARSLEY, PLACE IT IN A GLASS JAR WITH A SMALL AMOUNT OF WATER. COVER THE JAR TIGHTLY, REFRIGERATE, AND CHANGE WATER EVERY FIVE DAYS.

PEAR SALAD

> 1 pear, thinly sliced
>
> 3 cups spring salad mix
>
> ½ cup Balsamic Dressing (recipe follows)
>
> ½ cup Sugared Pecans (page 40)

In medium bowl, combine pear and salad, toss to mix. Drizzle with dressing. Top with pecans.

Balsamic Dressing

> 2 tablespoons plus 2 teaspoons balsamic vinegar
>
> 2 tablespoons olive oil
>
> 2 tablespoons water
>
> ¼ teaspoon garlic salt
>
> ¼ teaspoon dried basil
>
> ¼ teaspoon dried oregano

In small bowl, combine all ingredients. Mix well.

ROMAINE SALAD

> ½ head romaine lettuce, chopped
>
> ½ cup white beans, drained, rinsed
>
> 3 tablespoons chopped, sun dried tomatoes packed in olive oil
>
> Red Wine Vinaigrette (recipe follows)

In medium bowl, place lettuce. Top with beans and tomatoes. Serve with dressing.

Red Wine Vinaigrette

     4 teaspoons red wine vinegar

     3 tablespoons olive oil

     ¼ teaspoon salt

     ⅛ teaspoon pepper

In small bowl, combine all ingredients. Mix well.

IT'S A DATE SALAD

     2 cups mixed green lettuce

     3 dried dates, chopped

     ¼ cup crumbled soft goat cheese

     2 tablespoons chopped walnuts

     Soy Sauce Vinaigrette (recipe follows)

In medium bowl, place salad. Top with dates, cheese, and walnuts. Serve with Soy Sauce Vinaigrette.

Soy Sauce Vinaigrette

     ½ cup olive oil

     2 tablespoons red wine vinegar

     1 tablespoon soy sauce

     ¼ teaspoon pepper

In small bowl, combine all ingredients. Mix well.

SOUTHERN COLESLAW

2 cups shredded cabbage
1 carrot, peeled, grated
½ cup mayonnaise
1 tablespoon apple cider vinegar
1 tablespoon sugar

In medium bowl, combine cabbage and carrot. In small bowl, combine remaining ingredients. Mix well. Pour mixture over cabbage, toss to coat. Cover. Chill 30 minutes.

PINEAPPLE COLESLAW

1½ cups shredded cabbage
⅓ cup pineapple tidbits, drained
⅓ cup diced apple
¼ cup diced celery
½ cup miniature marshmallows
⅓ cup Miracle Whip®

In large bowl, combine all ingredients. Mix well. Cover. Chill.

MIXED CABBAGE SLAW

1 cup shredded green cabbage
½ cup shredded red cabbage
¼ cup shredded carrots
⅓ cup Miracle Whip®
1 teaspoon sugar
1 teaspoon cider vinegar

In large bowl, combine green cabbage, red cabbage, and carrots. In small bowl, combine Miracle Whip, sugar, and vinegar. Mix well. Pour mixture over cabbage. Mix well.

SIDE DISH BEAN SALAD

1 cup kidney beans, drained
2 hard cooked eggs, peeled, chopped
1 tablespoon sweet relish
¼ cup chopped onions
1 teaspoon sugar
⅓ cup Miracle Whip®

In medium bowl, combine all ingredients. Mix well. Cover. Chill.

ITALIAN SALAD

1 tomato, chopped
½ cucumber, diced
¼ cup sliced olives
1 cup chickpeas
¾ cup shredded mozzarella cheese
Italian Dressing (recipe follows)

In medium bowl, combine all ingredients. Mix well.

Italian Dressing

¼ cup olive oil
3 tablespoons water
2 tablespoons white wine vinegar
1 teaspoon dried oregano
½ teaspoon Dijon mustard
1 clove garlic, minced

In small bowl, combine all ingredients. Mix well.

BROCCOLI SALAD

        2 cups broccoli florets
        ½ cup raisins
        ¼ cup chopped red onion
        ½ cup mayonnaise
        1 tablespoon cider vinegar
        1 tablespoon sugar

In medium bowl, combine broccoli, raisins, and onion. In small bowl, combine remaining ingredients. Mix well. Pour over broccoli, toss to coat.

ENTICING RICE SALAD

        ½ cup cooked rice
        ½ cup miniature marshmallows
        ½ cup pineapple tidbits
        ¼ cup coconut
        1 small apple, cored, diced
        1 cup whipped topping

In medium bowl, combine all ingredients. Mix well. Cover. Chill.

PINEAPPLE & STUFF SALAD

        1 cup cottage cheese
        ½ (4 serving) box any flavor Jell-O®
        ½ cup crushed pineapple
        ½ cup whipped topping

In medium bowl, add cottage cheese. Sprinkle Jell-O over top. Add pineapple and whipped topping. Mix well. Cover. Chill.

HONEY OF A SALAD

½ cup vanilla yogurt
1 tablespoon orange juice
1 tablespoon honey
¼ cup raisins
1 medium apple, cored, chopped

In medium bowl, combine yogurt, juice, and honey. Mix well. Add raisins and apples. Mix well. Cover. Chill.

YOGURT MELON SALAD

½ cup sliced strawberries
1 cup cubed cantaloupe
⅔ cup peach yogurt
Toasted coconut

In 2 serving dishes, combine strawberries and melon. Spoon yogurt over top. Sprinkle coconut over yogurt. Chill until serving time.

APPLE SALAD TAILORED FOR TWO

1 large apple, cored, cubed
½ cup sliced grapes
1 small banana, chopped
1 cup miniature marshmallows
¼ cup chopped walnuts (optional)
1¼ cups whipped topping

In medium bowl, combine all ingredients. Mix well. Chill.

NICE CHANGE FRUIT SALAD

½ cup orange juice

1 tablespoon sugar

1 tablespoon cornstarch

1 medium orange, peeled, chopped

1 medium apple, cored, chopped

1 small banana, sliced

In small saucepan, combine orange juice, sugar, and cornstarch. Over low heat cook and stir until sauce thickens. Remove from heat. Cool. In medium bowl, combine all fruit. Pour sauce over fruit. Mix well. Cover. Chill.

RIGHT TOUCH APPLE SALAD

1 medium apple, cored, cubed

½ cup sliced grapes

1 small celery stalk, chopped

¼ cup chopped walnuts

⅓ cup Miracle Whip®

1 teaspoon sugar

In medium bowl, combine all ingredients. Mix well. Cover. Chill 1 hour.

IT'S ONLY FRUIT & CHEESE SALAD

1 cup cottage cheese

½ cup sliced pears, drained

2 tablespoons shredded cheddar cheese

Place ½ cup cottage cheese on 2 plates, top evenly with pears. Sprinkle cheddar cheese over top.

CITRUS SALAD

1 grapefruit, peeled, chopped
1 orange, peeled, chopped
1 cup halved seedless grapes
2 tablespoons shredded coconut

In medium bowl, combine grapefruit, orange, and grapes. Mix well. Top with coconut.

MANDARIN CUCUMBER SALAD

¼ cup sugar
¼ cup water
¼ cup red wine vinegar
1 clove garlic, minced
¼ teaspoon red pepper flakes
1 cucumber, sliced, seeded
½ cup Mandarin oranges

In small saucepan, combine sugar, water, vinegar, garlic, and pepper flakes. Over medium high heat bring to a boil. Boil until sugar melts. Place cucumber and oranges in medium bowl. Pour mixture over cucumbers. Cover. Chill at least 2 hours.

TO GET THE MOST JUICE FROM A FRESH LEMON,
ROLL IT FIRMLY ON A COUNTERTOP, THEN MICRO-
WAVE IT ON HIGH FOR 20 SECONDS, OR SUBMERGE
IN HOT WATER FOR 15 MINUTES.

CRAB PASTA SALAD

½ cup uncooked macaroni shells
½ cup chopped imitation crab
½ cup chopped fresh baby spinach
¼ cup peas
2 tablespoons feta cheese
¼ cup Italian salad dressing

Cook pasta according to package directions. Drain. In medium bowl, combine all ingredients. Toss to coat.

SUMMERTIME PASTA SALAD

1 ½ cups uncooked spiral pasta
½ cup chopped broccoli
½ cup chopped cucumber
¼ cup chopped tomato
1 cup Ranch dressing

Cook pasta according to package directions. Drain. Rinse with cold water. In medium bowl, combine all ingredients. Mix well.

ORZO PASTA SALAD

¾ cup uncooked orzo pasta
½ cup chopped canned green beans
¼ cup Greek vinaigrette dressing
1 tomato, seeded, chopped
½ teaspoon lemon juice

Cook pasta according to package directions. Drain. Rinse in cold water. In medium bowl, combine all ingredients. Mix well.

TORTELLINI FOR BRUNCH SALAD

1½ cups frozen tortellini, cooked

6 cherry tomatoes, halved

¼ cup sliced green onions

⅓ cup creamy Italian dressing

In medium bowl, combine all ingredients. Mix well.

CHICKEN N MAC SALAD

½ cup chopped cooked chicken

2 cups cooked macaroni

1 stalk celery, chopped

1 green onion, chopped

½ cup Miracle Whip®

1 teaspoon sugar

In medium bowl, combine all ingredients. Mix well. Chill before serving.

DRESSING TO THE RESCUE

2 tablespoons salad oil

2 tablespoons vinegar

1½ teaspoons sugar

¼ teaspoon celery seed

⅛ teaspoon dry mustard

In jar, combine all ingredients. Cover. Shake well. Serve over salad.

VINAIGRETTE DRESSING

> 3 tablespoons vinegar
> 2 tablespoons sugar
> 2 tablespoons salad oil
> ½ teaspoon salt

In small bowl, combine all ingredients. Mix well. Serve over salad.

POUR OVER SALAD DRESSING

> ½ cup honey
> ½ teaspoon salt
> ⅓ cup wine vinegar
> 1 cup salad oil
> 1 tablespoon poppy seeds

In small bowl, combine honey, salt, and vinegar. Gradually add oil, stirring constantly. Add poppy seeds. Pour into covered container and refrigerate. Mix well before serving.

NOTES

Just Enough for Two

Main Dishes

WALK ABOUT TACOS

Fun to eat!

½ pound ground beef

2 tablespoons taco seasoning

2 tablespoons water

2 (1 ounce) packages Doritos® chips

3 tablespoons chopped onions

½ cup shredded cheddar cheese

1 cup shredded lettuce

In medium saucepan, add ground beef. Over medium heat cook and crumble beef until browned. Drain. Add taco seasoning and water. Reduce heat to low simmer 3 to 4 minutes. Open Doritos and squeeze bags lightly. Spoon ground beef, onions, cheese, and lettuce evenly in Doritos bags.

Note: Top with any favorite toppings. Walk and eat at the same time.

AN EASY FIX FOR TAMALES

1 (15 ounce) can tamales, cut in 2-inch pieces

1 cup chili without beans

⅓ cup chopped onions

1 cup chopped corn chips

⅔ cup shredded Mexican cheese

Preheat oven to 350 degrees. In 1½-quart baking dish, layer tamales. Cover with chili and onions. Sprinkle chips and cheese over chili. Cover. Bake 20 to 30 minutes.

PITA POCKETS PIZZA

2 pita pockets
1 cup cooked ground beef
½ cup pizza sauce
½ cup shredded mozzarella cheese
1 cup shredded lettuce

Preheat oven to 400 degrees. Place pitas on baking sheet, divide ground beef, sauce, and cheese evenly on pitas. Bake 8 to 10 minutes. Top with lettuce.

COUNTRY PORK SKILLET

2 boneless pork loin chops, diced
1 (12 ounce) jar pork gravy
1 tablespoon ketchup
4 small red potatoes, diced
1 cup frozen mixed vegetables

In medium skillet, add pork, brown over medium heat. Stir in gravy, ketchup, and potatoes. Mix well. Cover. Cook on low 10 minutes. Add vegetables. Cover. Cook 15 minutes.

HAM & VEGGIE
SLOW COOKER SUPPER

1½ cups frozen O'Brien potatoes
½ cup chopped cooked ham
¾ cup shredded cheddar cheese
1 cup frozen green beans
1 (10¾ ounce) can cream of potato soup
¼ cup sour cream

In 3-quart slow cooker, combine all ingredients, except sour cream. Cover. Cook on low 5 to 6 hours. Stir in sour cream. Cover. Cook 5 minutes.

HAM & BEANS

1 cup water
¼ cup diced ham
1 cup butterbeans, soaked overnight, drain, rinse
⅛ teaspoon salt
⅛ teaspoon pepper
1 tablespoon butter

In small saucepan, add water and ham. Over medium high heat bring to a boil. Reduce heat to low. Cook 5 minutes. Add beans, salt and pepper. Cover. Simmer 45 minutes, or until beans are tender. Add more water if needed. Add butter. Mix well.

QUICK PINTO BEANS & SAUSAGE

1 (15 ounce) can pinto beans, undrained
1 smoked link sausage, sliced
¼ cup water
½ teaspoon Cajun seasoning
Hot rice

In medium saucepan, combine all ingredients, except rice. Mix well. Over low heat cook 15 minutes. Serve over cooked rice

ITALIAN SAUSAGE SANDWICH

½ pound mild Italian sausage
2 French sub rolls, split
¼ cup sliced mild pepper rings
1 cup shredded mozzarella

Preheat oven to broil. Shape sausage into two patties, to fit rolls when cooked. In large skillet, brown sausage over medium high heat, until fully cooked. Place rolls on baking sheet. Top each roll with sausage. Arrange peppers over sausage. Sprinkle cheese over sausage and bun. Broil until cheese is melted and slightly golden brown.

TO SHRED CHEESE EASILY, PLACE
WRAPPED CHEESE IN FREEZER FOR TEN
MINUTES BEFORE SHREDDING.

PHILLY CHEESE SANDWICH

½ onion, thinly sliced
½ green bell pepper, thinly sliced
1 teaspoon butter or margarine
2 French sub rolls, split
4 ounces deli sliced roast beef
4 provolone cheese slices

Preheat oven to broil. In large skillet, brown onions and pepper in butter, over medium high heat. On baking sheet, place rolls cut side up. Layer beef, onion mixture, and cheese on each roll. Broil until cheese has melted.

CORDON BLEU PANINI

4 slices sourdough bread
4 tablespoons butter or margarine, softened
4 slices Swiss cheese
4 slices chicken luncheon meat
4 slices ham luncheon meat

Butter outside of each bread slice. Layer 1 slice cheese, 2 slices chicken, 2 slices ham, 1 slice cheese, and bread, butter side up. Repeat for second sandwich. Cook on contact grill, until golden brown.

GRILLED HAM SANDWICH

2 tablespoons Thousand Island salad dressing
½ teaspoon mustard
½ cup shredded coleslaw mix
1 tablespoon butter or margarine
4 slices sour dough bread
4 ounces deli sliced ham
2 slices Swiss cheese

In small bowl, combine dressing and mustard. Add coleslaw. Mix well. Butter one side of each bread slice. In large skillet, place 2 slices of bread, buttered side down. On bread slices, layer ham, coleslaw mixture, cheese, and remaining bread slice butter side up. Over medium high heat brown both sides.

Cooking Tip: Use your contact grill to cook sandwiches.

GREEN CHILE GRILLED CHEESE SANDWICH

1 tablespoon butter or margarine
4 slices sandwich bread
4 slices American cheese
2 tablespoons canned diced green chile

Butter one side of each bread slice. In large skillet, place 2 slices of bread, butter side down. On each bread slice in skillet, layer 1 slice American cheese, 1 tablespoon green chile, 1 slice American cheese, and remaining bread slice butter side up. Over medium high heat brown both sides.

PATTY MELT

½ pound ground beef, form 2 patties
1 medium onion, sliced
2 tablespoons butter
2 slices Swiss or mozzarella cheese
4 slices bread

In medium skillet, fry patties over medium heat to desired doneness. In small skillet, sauté onion in 1 tablespoon butter over medium high heat, until golden brown. Butter one side of each slice of bread. On 2 slices of bread butter side down, layer patties, cheese, onions, top with remaining bread slices. In medium skillet, cook sandwiches over medium heat until golden brown.

TURKEY MELT

1 medium onion, sliced
2 tablespoons butter or margarine
4 slices sourdough bread
2 tablespoons barbeque sauce
4 slices Monterey Jack cheese
8 slices cooked turkey

In medium skillet, sauté onions in 1 tablespoon butter over medium high heat. Cook until golden. Butter one side of each bread slice. Spread inside of bread with barbeque sauce. Layer cheese and turkey on 2 slices of bread, top with remaining slices. In large skillet, cook sandwiches over medium heat until golden brown.

HEALTH NUT SANDWICHES

4 slices multigrain bread
1 tablespoon Ranch dressing
8 ounces deli turkey slices
2 slices Provolone cheese
1 small avocado, sliced
½ cup alfalfa sprouts

Spread Ranch dressing on 2 slices bread. Layer each with remaining ingredients. Top with bread slices.

HAM SALAD SANDWICHES

¼ pound cooked ham, chopped
1 tablespoon minced onion
1 teaspoon dill pickle relish
1 tablespoon Miracle Whip®
¼ teaspoon mustard
4 slices sandwich bread

Place ham in blender or food processor, pulse until coarse. Add onion and relish, pulse to blend. Place mixture in small bowl. Add Miracle Whip and mustard. Mix well. Spoon ham mixture onto two slices of bread. Top with remaining slices.

TO KEEP A WOODEN CUTTING BOARD
FRESH, SPRINKLE WITH SALT AND THEN RUB
WITH LEMON

FRUITY TUNA SALAD SANDWICH

      1 (6 ounce) can tuna, drained
      ¼ cup diced apple
      2 tablespoons raisins
      2 tablespoons Miracle Whip®
      2 sandwich rolls, split

In small bowl, combine all ingredients except rolls. Mix well.
Spoon tuna mixture onto rolls. Garnish with lettuce if desired.

CHICKEN SALAD SANDWICHES

      1 cup shredded cooked chicken
      ¼ cup diced celery
      1 tablespoon Miracle Whip®
      1 tablespoon sour cream
      4 slices sandwich bread

In small bowl, combine all ingredients, except bread. Mix well.
Spread on 2 slices of bread. Top with remaining slices.

QUICK CHICKEN QUESADILLAS

4 (6-inch) flour tortillas
2 tablespoons butter
1 cup cooked shredded chicken
2 tablespoons diced green chile
¾ cup shredded cheddar cheese

Butter one side of each tortilla. In large skillet, place one tortilla butter side down. place ½ cup chicken, sprinkle 1 tablespoon green chile and ½ of cheese. Top with tortilla, butter side up. Over medium heat cook until golden. Flip. Cook until golden. Remove. Slice into wedges. Repeat process.

Cooking Tip: Use your contact grill.

CHICKEN SURPRISE QUESADILLAS

4 (6-inch) flour tortillas
2 tablespoons butter
1 chicken breast, cooked, diced
1 green apple, cored, chopped
¾ cup shredded Colby & Monterey Jack blend cheese
2 tablespoons salsa

Butter one side of each tortilla. In large skillet, place one tortilla butter side down. Layer half of chicken, apple, cheese and salsa on tortilla. Top with tortilla, butter side up. Cover. Cook over medium heat until golden. Flip. Cook until golden. Remove. Slice into wedges. Repeat process.

Cooking Tip: Use your contact grill.

CHICKEN WRAPS

2 (8-inch) flour tortillas

2 tablespoons Miracle Whip®

2 lettuce leaves

1 boneless, skinless, chicken breast, cooked, cut into strips

4 slices bacon, cooked

1 small tomato, chopped

Microwave tortillas 30 seconds. Spread Miracle Whip on tortillas. Layer lettuce, chicken, bacon, tomato on tortillas. Roll up. Secure with toothpicks, cut in half.

TACO CHICKEN WRAPS

1 cup diced chicken

½ teaspoon taco seasoning

2 (6-inch) flour tortillas

2 tablespoons salsa

¼ cup shredded cheddar cheese

In small skillet, place chicken, sprinkle with taco seasoning. Over medium heat brown until fully cooked. Microwave tortillas for 30 seconds. On each tortilla, layer chicken, salsa, and cheese. Roll up. Secure with toothpicks.

ALWAYS REMOVE DAMAGED OR BRUISED AREAS
FROM FRUITS AND VEGETABLES. THEY MAY
CONTAIN BACTERIA.

HOT HAM & CHEESE WRAPS

2 (6-inch) flour tortillas
4 slices smoked ham luncheon meat
2 slices American cheese
⅓ cup lettuce
¼ cup chopped tomato

Layer tortillas with ham and cheese. Microwave 30 seconds. Top with lettuce and tomato. Roll up. Secure with toothpicks. Cut in half. Serve warm.

CHICKEN PITAS

2 pita breads, halved, split
2 tablespoons onion cream cheese
1 chicken breast, cooked shredded
¼ cup chopped lettuce

Spread cream cheese inside pitas. Stuff with chicken and lettuce.

ONE DISH CHICKEN DINNER

1 (6 ounce) box one step chicken stuffing
1 cup hot water
1 large boneless, skinless, chicken breast,
cut into 1-inch pieces, browned
1 (10¾ ounce) can cream of chicken soup
⅓ cup sour cream
1 cup frozen vegetables, thawed, drained

Preheat oven to 400 degrees. In 1½-quart baking dish, sprinkle ½ cup dry stuffing evenly on bottom. Set aside. In medium bowl, combine remaining stuffing and water. Mix well. Place chicken over dry stuffing. In small bowl, combine soup, sour cream, and vegetables. Mix well. Spoon mixture over chicken. Top with stuffing. Bake 30 to 40 minutes.

BAKED HAM & SWEET POTATOES

2 ham steaks
1 (15 ounce) can sweet potatoes, drained
1 (8 ounce) can crushed pineapple, drained
¼ cup packed brown sugar
1 cup mini marshmallows

Preheat oven 350 degrees. In 9 x 13-inch baking dish, place ham. Top with sweet potatoes and pineapple. Sprinkle brown sugar on top. Cover with foil. Bake 30 minutes. Remove. Sprinkle marshmallows over top. Bake 10 minutes.

Cooking Note: Great dish for the holidays.

MICROWAVE STUFFED SQUASH

1 medium acorn squash, halved, seeded
½ pound pork sausage
¼ cup finely chopped onion
¼ cup finely chopped celery
2 tablespoons plus 2 teaspoons sour cream

Place squash cut side down on microwave safe plate. Microwave on high 10 to 13 minutes or until tender. In large skillet, crumble sausage, add onion and celery. Over medium heat cook until meat is browned. Drain. Add sour cream. Spoon into squash halves. Cover. Microwave 1 minute.

BEEF FAJITAS

½ pound beef sirloin steak, thinly sliced
¼ cup plus 2 tablespoons Italian dressing, divided
1 medium green bell pepper, sliced thin
1 small onion, sliced thin
4 (6-inch) flour tortillas
½ cup shredded cheddar cheese

In large resealable plastic bag, combine steak and ¼ cup dressing. Toss to coat. Refrigerate 1 hour, turn bag after 30 minutes. Discard marinade. In large skillet, brown steak in 2 tablespoons dressing, over medium high heat to desired doneness. Remove meat. Add pepper and onion, cook until golden brown. Add steak, cook 1 minute. Microwave tortillas for 30 seconds. Layer on tortillas, steak and vegetables, top with cheese. Garnish with sour cream, guacamole, and salsa if desired.

MEXICAN CHILI DOGS

4 (6-inch) corn tortillas

4 hotdogs

½ cup chili

½ cup thick and chunky salsa

½ cup shredded cheddar cheese

Preheat oven to 350 degrees. On each tortilla, place hotdog and 2 tablespoons chili. Roll up. Place seam down in 9 x 9-inch greased baking dish. Spread salsa over tortillas. Cover. Bake 25 minutes. Uncover. Sprinkle with cheese, bake 5 minutes or until cheese is melted.

MEXI MAC & CHEESE

1 cup double cheddar cheese sauce

½ cup mild salsa

2 cups cooked macaroni

In medium saucepan, combine all ingredients. Mix well. Over medium heat cook until hot.

DOCTORED UP MAC & CHEESE

1 pound purchased deli macaroni and cheese

¼ cup sliced marinated sun dried tomatoes

¼ cup real bacon bits

3 tablespoons seasoned bread crumbs

1 tablespoon butter or margarine, melted

Preheat oven to 375 degrees. In medium bowl, combine macaroni and cheese, tomatoes, and bacon. Mix well. Pour mixture into greased 1-quart baking dish. In small bowl, combine crumbs and butter. Mix well. Sprinkle on top of macaroni mixture. Bake 20 to 25 minutes or until golden brown.

BEEF GOULASH

1½ cups cooked ground beef
½ cup chopped tomatoes
½ cup tomato sauce
2 tablespoons diced onion
2 cups cooked macaroni
½ teaspoon salt

In medium saucepan, combine all ingredients. Mix well. Over low heat cook 15 minutes.

IT'S QUICK & EASY TORTELLINI

1 (9 ounce) package refrigerated chicken filled tortellini
½ cup frozen sweet peas
¾ cup half-and-half
¼ cup grated parmesan cheese
2 tablespoons cream cheese

In medium saucepan, combine tortellini and peas. Cook as directed on tortellini package. Drain. Keep warm. In small saucepan, combine half-and-half, parmesan cheese, and cream cheese. Over low heat cook, stirring until smooth and hot. Stir in cooked tortellini and peas. Cook 2 to 3 minutes.

IF YOU ONLY NEED ONE-HALF AN ONION,
SAVE THE ROOT HALF. IT WILL KEEP
LONGER.

RAVIOLI WITH TOMATOES

    1 (9 ounce) package cheese filled ravioli
    1 (14.5 ounce) can diced tomatoes with
        basil, garlic, and oregano, undrained
    2 tablespoons parmesan cheese

Cook ravioli as directed on package. Drain. Combine remaining ingredients. Mix well. Over low heat simmer until hot.

HAMBURGER STROGANOFF

    6 ounces ground beef
    1 (10¾ ounce) can mushroom soup
    ¾ cup milk
    1 tablespoon ketchup
    2 tablespoons sour cream
    Hot noodles

In medium saucepan, brown beef. Add soup, milk, and ketchup. Over low heat simmer 10 minutes. Add sour cream. Mix well. Serve over noodles.

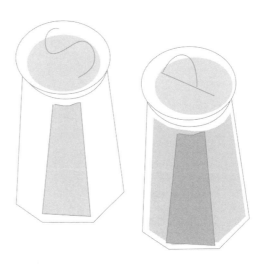

BEEF STROGANOFF ON NOODLES

1 tablespoons margarine

½ pound sirloin steak, sliced thin

¼ teaspoon garlic salt

1 cup sliced mushrooms

¼ cup beef broth

1 tablespoon ketchup

¼ cup chive and onion sour cream

Hot noodles

In medium skillet, melt margarine over medium heat. Add beef, cook 3 minutes. Sprinkle salt over beef. Add mushrooms, broth, ketchup, and sour cream, cook 5 minutes, stirring frequently. Serve over hot noodles.

LAST MINUTE TUNA CASSEROLE

1 (6 ounce) can white tuna, drained

2 cups cooked noodles

2 tablespoons butter

1 (10¾ ounce) can cream of mushroom soup

½ cup milk

¼ cup shredded mozzarella cheese

Preheat oven to 350 degrees. In medium bowl, combine all ingredients. Mix well. Pour mixture into 2-quart baking dish. Bake 20 to 30 minutes.

STIR IN FETTUCCINE

1 (4.7 ounce) box fettuccine

6 ounce sirloin steak, cooked, sliced

½ cup small broccoli florets

1 small tomato, chopped

Prepare fettuccine according to directions on box. Add remaining ingredients with fettuccine. Over low heat cook 5 minutes or until hot.

HAM & CHEESE FETTUCCINE

6 ounces fettuccine

1½ cups cubed cooked ham

1 cup frozen peas, thawed

1 cup grated parmesan cheese

½ cup heavy whipping cream

Cook pasta according to package directions. Drain. In large saucepan, add ham, peas, cheese, and cream. Over medium heat cook until cheese has melted. Add fettuccine. Mix well.

GARLIC PASTA

4 ounces spaghetti, uncooked

2 tablespoons olive oil

2 tablespoons butter or margarine

3 cloves garlic, minced

2 tablespoons lemon juice

Cook spaghetti according to package directions, drain. In medium skillet, heat oil and butter over medium high heat. Add garlic, cook 1 minute. Add lemon juice. Cook 1 minute. Add spaghetti, toss to coat.

TILAPIA LINGUINE

6 ounces linguine

½ cup Alfredo sauce

2 tilapia filets

8 leaves spinach

Prepare linguine according to package direction. Grill or fry tilapia until cooked and flakey, about 4 minutes on each side. On two plates layer on each, ½ of linguine, 2 tablespoons sauce, ½ of spinach, 1 tilapia fillet, and remaining sauce.

GREEN CHILE CHICKEN PASTA

1 boneless, skinless chicken breast, cooked, diced

2 cups Alfredo sauce

4 ounces pasta, cooked, drained

2 tablespoons diced green chile

1 cup shredded Monterey jack cheese

Preheat oven to 350 degrees. In 1-quart baking dish, combine all ingredients, except cheese. Mix well. Sprinkle cheese on top. Bake 30 minutes.

**TO REHEAT COOKED PASTA, PLACE IT IN A
COLANDER AND RUN HOT WATER OVER IT.**

BUTTER NOODLES

4 ounces egg noodles
2 tablespoons butter or margarine
⅛ teaspoon garlic powder
2 tablespoons grated Parmesan cheese

Cook pasta according to package directions. Drain. Add butter and garlic powder. Toss to coat. Place in 2 bowls, top with cheese.

STIR-FRY CHICKEN PASTA

3 cups (6 ounces) uncooked egg noodles
½ cup frozen sugar snaps peas
1 cup cooked, chopped chicken, warm
½ cup stir-fry sauce
2 tablespoons honey

Cook pasta according to package directions, add peas during last 3 minutes of cooking. Drain. Add remaining ingredients. Toss to coat.

PEAS & PASTA

4 ounces spinach linguine, uncooked
1 cup chicken broth
1 cup whipping cream
½ cup grated parmesan cheese
½ cup frozen peas, thawed
3 slices bacon, cooked, crumbled

Cook pasta according to package directions. In small saucepan, add broth and cream. Over medium high heat bring to a boil. Reduce heat to low. Simmer 25 minutes. Add cheese, peas, and bacon. Cook until cheese melts. Toss with linguine.

LINGUINI IN CLAM SAUCE

   1½ cups pasta sauce

   1 (6½ ounce) can chopped clams, undrained

   ⅛ teaspoon crushed red pepper flakes

   2 cups cooked linguini

In small saucepan, combine all ingredients, except linguini. Mix well. Over medium heat bring mixture to a boil. Reduce heat to low. Simmer uncovered 5 minutes. Spoon mixture over hot linguini.

SKIP-A-STEP SPAGHETTI

   ½ pound ground beef

   ¼ cup chopped onions

   2 tablespoons chopped green bell pepper

   2 cups pasta sauce

   Cooked spaghetti

In medium skillet, combine beef and onions, brown over medium heat. Drain. Add remaining ingredients, except spaghetti. Mix well. Cook on low 10 minutes. Serve with spaghetti.

LASAGNA

5 lasagna noodles

½ pound ground beef

1 (14 ounce) jar spaghetti sauce

¾ cup ricotta cheese

1 egg, beaten

1 cup shredded mozzarella cheese

Preheat oven to 350 degrees. Cook noodles according to package directions. Drain. In large skillet, brown beef over medium high heat. Drain. Add spaghetti sauce. Over low heat cook 5 minutes. In small bowl, combine ricotta cheese and egg. Mix well. In greased 8 x 4 x 2-inch loaf pan, spread ¼ cup meat sauce. Place 2 noodles over sauce. Layer with ⅓ of cheese mixture, ⅓ remaining meat sauce, and ⅓ mozzarella cheese. Repeat layering 2 more times. Bake 30 to 35 minutes.

RICH ALFREDO SAUCE

¼ cup butter

4 ounces cream cheese

1 teaspoon garlic powder

1 cup milk

3 ounces grated parmesan cheese.

In small saucepan, melt butter over medium heat. Add cream cheese and garlic powder. Whisk until smooth. Slowly add milk, stirring constantly, until smooth. Add cheese. Whisk until smooth. Add additional milk if too thick.

SPAGHETTI SAUCE

¼ cup diced onion

1 clove garlic, minced

2 tablespoons olive oil

1 (8 ounce) can tomato sauce

¼ teaspoon dried basil

In medium saucepan, add onion and garlic in oil. Over medium heat cook until tender. Add remaining ingredients. Cook 2 minutes. Reduce heat to low. Cover. Simmer 10 minutes.

HASH BROWN CASSEROLE

2 cups frozen diced hash browns with peppers and onions

1 tablespoon butter or margarine

1 cup diced smoked sausage

¼ cup shredded cheddar cheese

In large skillet, brown hash browns in butter over medium high heat. Add sausage during last 5 minutes of cooking. Remove from heat. Sprinkle cheese on top. Cover with lid until cheese melts.

SUNDAY BRUNCH CASSEROLE

2 slices bread, torn into pieces

6 ounces bacon or sausage, cooked, crumbled

1 cup shredded cheddar cheese

3 eggs

1 cup milk

Preheat oven 350 degrees. Spray 9 x 9-inch baking dish with cooking spray. Arrange bread in bottom. Sprinkle meat and cheese over bread. In small bowl, combine eggs and milk. If desired add salt and pepper. Mix well. Pour over cheese. Bake 35 to 40 minutes.

SUNDAY MORNING EGG CUPS

2 cups frozen hash browns, thawed

¼ cup chopped green onions

¼ teaspoon seasoned salt

¾ cup shredded cheddar cheese

2 eggs

Preheat oven to 400 degrees. In two ovenproof bowls, coat with cooking spray. In medium bowl, combine hash browns, green onions, salt, and cheese. Mix well. Press mixture in bottom and up side of each bowl. Bake 25 to 30 minutes or until golden and crisp. Remove from oven. Break egg into center of each cup. Bake 8 to 10 minutes or until eggs are set.

BED & BREAKFAST SCRAMBLED EGGS

4 slices bread, crusts removed
2 tablespoons butter
3 eggs, beaten
¼ cup diced ham
salt and pepper
½ cup shredded cheddar cheese

Use rolling pin to flatten bread. Spread teaspoon of butter over one side of each slice. Press buttered side down into four muffin cups. Bake for 10 minutes or until golden brown. In small bowl, combine eggs, ham, salt, and pepper. In small skillet with remaining butter, add egg mixture. Over medium heat cook until eggs are set. Spoon mixture into bread cups. Sprinkle with cheese. Bake 2 minutes or until cheese melts.

FRENCH VANILLA BLUEBERRY OATMEAL

1½ cups water
1 cup quick cooking oats
⅓ cup sugar
½ cup blueberries (thaw if frozen)
1½ tablespoons French vanilla coffee creamer

In small saucepan add water. Over medium high heat bring to boil. Stir in oats and sugar, cook 1 minute. Remove from heat. Fold in blueberries and creamer.

NOTES

Just Enough for Two

Meats

COUNTRY-STYLE RIBS

1 small onion, sliced

¼ cup maple syrup

2 tablespoons spicy brown mustard

1½ pounds country style ribs, fat trimmed

In 3-quart slow cooker, place onions. In small bowl, combine syrup and mustard. Mix well. Spread mixture over ribs. Place ribs on onions. Cover. Cook on low 6 to 8 hours.

SWISS STEAK FOR DINNER

¾ pound beef round steak, browned, cut in half

6 new potatoes cut into quarters

1 large carrot, sliced

1 (14½ ounce) can diced tomatoes with basil, garlic, and oregano

In 3-quart slow cooker, combine all ingredients. Cover. Cook on low 6 to 8 hours.

SLOW COOKED BRISKET

1 pound boneless beef brisket

1 small onion, sliced

1 (10¾ ounce) can cream of celery soup

¼ cup water

In 3-quart slow cooker, place brisket. Add onions on top. In small bowl, combine soup and water. Pour mixture over brisket. Cover. Cook on low 7 to 8 hours.

SUNDAY DINNER ROAST

2 medium potatoes, peeled, cut into quarters

1 carrot, sliced

1 small onion, sliced

1 tablespoon margarine

1 tablespoon oil

½ teaspoon salt

1 pound roast

½ cup water

In 3-quart slow cooker, add potatoes, carrots, and onions. In medium skillet, add margarine and oil. Salt roast. Place in skillet. Over medium heat brown both sides of roast. Place on vegetables. Add water to same skillet. Bring to a boil. Pour over roast. Cover. Cook on low 8 to 10 hours or bake at 350 degrees 1½ to 2 hours.

MARINATED STEAKS

¼ cup Balsamic vinegar

¼ cup soy sauce

¼ cup Worchester sauce

2 rib eye steaks

In large resealable plastic bag, combine vinegar, soy sauce, and Worchester. Toss to mix. Add steaks. Refrigerate at least 1 hour, turning after 30 minutes. Discard marinade. Grill to desired doneness.

FILET MIGNON

½ tablespoon butter
½ teaspoon vegetable oil
2 (4 to 6 ounce) filet mignon steaks
½ teaspoon pepper
½ teaspoon garlic salt

In medium skillet, heat butter and oil over medium heat until hot. Sprinkle steaks with pepper and garlic salt, place in skillet. Cook until desired doneness.

TROPICAL T-BONE

¼ cup pineapple preserves
2 tablespoons teriyaki basting sauce
1 teaspoon lemon juice
1 teaspoon steak seasoning
2 T-bone steaks

In small saucepan, combine preserves, teriyaki, and lemon juice, cook over low heat until preserves have melted. Season steak. Grill steaks over medium heat to desired doneness, brushing with pineapple glaze during the last 2 minutes of cooking.

LET BEEF STAND A FEW MINUTES AFTER GRILLING. IT WILL BE TASTIER.

THYME FOR SIRLOIN

2 tablespoons steak sauce
1 clove garlic, minced
¼ teaspoon pepper
¼ teaspoon dried thyme leaves
½ pound boneless beef sirloin steak

In small bowl, combine all ingredients, except steak, mix well. Brush both sides of steak with sauce. Grill over medium heat, until desired doneness, brushing with sauce twice during cooking. Slice before serving.

THREE PEPPER STEAK

1 tablespoon steak seasoning
2 (6 ounce) beef top loin steak
½ small green bell pepper, cut in thin strips
½ small yellow bell pepper, cut in thin strips
½ small red bell pepper, cut in thin strips
1 tablespoon butter or margarine

Sprinkle seasoning on steak. Grill or broil steaks to desired doneness. In large skillet, sauté peppers in butter until tender, over medium high heat. Top each steak with peppers.

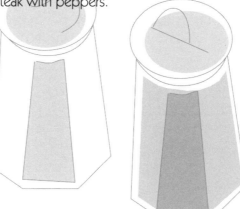

BEEF STIR FRY

    1 tablespoon oil
    ½ pound top sirloin steak, cut in 1 inch strips
    1 small onion, sliced
1½ cups fresh broccoli florets
    1 small red bell pepper, sliced
    ⅓ cup stir fry sauce

In medium skillet with oil, add steak. Over medium heat cook until brown. Add remaining ingredients. Cover. Cook 5 to 6 minutes or until vegetables are crisp tender.

FRIED STEAK STRIPS

½ pound round steak, cut into 1 inch strips
¼ cup milk
 1 egg
¾ cup flour
Salt and pepper
Oil for frying

In small bowl, combine milk and egg, mix well. Dredge steak in flour. Dip in egg. Dredge in flour again. Salt and pepper to taste. Set aside. In large skillet, add oil to ½ inch deep, heat over medium high heat. Fry steak in hot oil until golden brown.

BACKYARD PICNIC RIBS

¼ cup minced onion

1 tablespoon minced garlic

½ cup ketchup

¼ cup chili sauce

1 tablespoon packed brown sugar

1 pound beef ribs

In small saucepan, combine all ingredients, except ribs. Mix well. Over low heat cook 8 minutes. Baste ribs with mixture. Place on grill. Cook 30 to 40 minutes, basting ribs occasionally.

TASTY VEAL CUTLETS

2 veal cutlets

1 egg, beaten

½ cup Italian style bread crumbs

1 tablespoon oil

1 (8 ounce) can tomato sauce

½ cup shredded mozzarella cheese

Dip each veal cutlet into egg, coat with bread crumbs. In medium skillet with oil, place veal. Over medium heat brown both sides of veal. Add tomato sauce. Reduce heat to low. Cover. Cook on low until veal is tender. Sprinkle cheese over top. Cook 3 minutes.

ROAST BEEF AU JUS

1 pound rump roast
2 cloves garlic, peeled
1 small onion, sliced
⅓ cup beef broth
Rolls

Make 2 slits deep into beef roast. Insert garlic into slits. Coat a 3-quart slow cooker with cooking spray. Place onions in slow cooker. Pour broth over onions. Place roast on onions. Cover. Cook on low 6 to 8 hours. Remove roast, place on cutting board. Slice roast. Serve on rolls, split and toasted. Cover rolls with beef, onion, and juice.

SLOW COOKER CHUCK ROAST

1 pound boneless beef chuck roast
½ cup water
¾ cup tomato sauce
½ cup chopped tomatoes

In 3-quart slow cooker, place roast. In small bowl, combine water, tomato sauce, and chopped tomatoes. Mix well. Pour mixture over roast. Cover. Cook on low 6 to 8 hours.

THE HUMPTY DUMPTY DRIVE INN IN DENVER, COLORADO, TRADEMARKED THE NAME CHEESEBURGER IN 1935.

SPICE UP POT ROAST

1½ pounds boneless beef roast
6 tablespoons chili sauce
1 (12 ounce) can cola

In 3-quart slow cooker, place roast. In small bowl, combine chili sauce and cola. Pour mixture over roast. Cover. Cook on low 6 to 8 hours.

SO EASY MEAT LOAF

½ pound ground beef
1 egg
⅓ cup chopped onion
¼ cup diced celery
1 cup ketchup
½ cup cracker crumbs

Preheat oven to 350 degrees. In large bowl, combine beef, egg, onion, celery, ½ cup ketchup, and cracker crumbs. Mix well. Shape into loaf. Place in 1½-quart baking dish. Spread remaining ketchup over top. Bake 25 to 30 minutes.

A FAVORITE MEAT LOAF

1 pound lean ground beef

1 egg

½ cup bread crumbs

¼ cup chopped onions

¼ cup ketchup

2 tablespoons diced green bell pepper

½ teaspoon pepper

½ teaspoon salt

⅓ cup ketchup

Preheat oven to 350 degrees. In large bowl, combine all ingredients, except ⅓ cup ketchup. Mix well. Shape mixture into loaf. Place in 2-quart baking dish coated with cooking spray. Spread ketchup over loaf. Bake 30 to 40 minutes.

MEAT & POTATOES LOAF

½ pound ground beef

2 teaspoons dry onion soup mix

1 small potato, shredded

⅛ cup chopped mushrooms

⅛ cup mozzarella cheese

¼ cup ketchup

Preheat oven 350 degrees. In medium bowl, combine beef and soup mix. Mix well. In baking dish, place ½ meat mixture, make a well in the center to 1 inch from edge. In small bowl, combine potato, mushrooms, and cheese. Spread in well. Top with remaining meat mixture. Seal edges. Bake 30 minutes. Spread ketchup on top, bake 15 minutes.

MEXICAN MEATLOAF

½ pound ground beef
1 cup canned kidney beans, drained
1½ teaspoon taco seasoning
1 cup crushed corn tortillas
1 egg
½ cup chunky salsa

Preheat oven to 350 degrees. In large bowl, combine beef, beans, seasoning, tortillas, and egg. Mix well. In loaf pan, form meat mixture into loaf shape. Bake 30 minutes. Top with salsa, bake 15 minutes.

POTATO CHIP BURGERS

¾ pound ground beef
¼ cup crushed sour cream and onion potato chips
¼ cup barbecue sauce
2 buns

In medium bowl, combine all ingredients, except buns. Mix well. Shape into 2 patties. Grill until done.

SIMPLE HAMBURGERS

¾ pound ground beef
2 tablespoons brown gravy mix
⅛ teaspoon pepper

In medium bowl, combine all ingredients. Mix well. Shape into 2 patties. Broil or grill until done.

BEER BEEF BURGERS

½ pound ground beef
½ cup beer
½ teaspoon yellow mustard
Salt & pepper to taste
2 buns

In medium skillet, crumble and brown beef over medium high heat. Drain. Add remaining ingredients. Cook until liquid evaporates. Spoon onto buns.

ONION BURGERS

½ pound ground beef
¾ cup crushed French fried onions
2 tablespoons Worchester sauce
2 hamburger buns
2 slices American cheese

In medium bowl, combine beef, onions, and Worcestershire sauce. Mix well. Shape into 2 patties. Grill or fry to desired doneness. Place on buns, top with cheese.

GREEK BURGERS

½ pound ground turkey
½ cup crumbled feta cheese
1 teaspoon dried oregano
2 hamburger buns

In medium bowl, combine turkey, cheese, and oregano. Mix well. Shape into 2 patties. Grill or fry patties to desired doneness. Place on buns. Garnish with sliced olives and Greek salad dressing if desired.

HAWAIIAN BACON BURGER

½ pound ground beef, shape into 2 patties
2 tablespoons honey barbeque sauce
2 pineapple slices, grilled
4 slices bacon, cooked
2 hamburger buns

Place ground beef patties on grill. Baste with barbeque sauce when cooked halfway. Cook to desired doneness. Place on buns. Top each with grilled pineapple and 2 slices of bacon.

WHAT A FLAKE BURGER

½ pound ground beef
2 tablespoons instant potato flakes
1 teaspoon meatloaf seasoning mix
2 hamburger buns

In medium bowl, combine all ingredients, except buns. Mix well. Shape into 2 patties. Grill or fry to desired doneness. Place on buns.

QUICK TO MAKE MEATBALLS

½ pound lean ground beef
⅓ cup Italian seasoned dry bread crumbs
1 small egg
1 (16 ounce) jar pasta sauce

In medium bowl, combine all ingredients, except pasta sauce. Mix well. Shape into 6 meatballs. Place in 3-quart slow cooker. Pour sauce over meatballs. Cover. Cook on low 5 to 6 hours. Serve over spaghetti or make Hero Meatball Sandwiches.

DISH UP SAUSAGE & PEPPERS

1 tablespoon olive oil

¾ pound Italian sausage, sliced

1 small green bell pepper, sliced

1½ cups pasta sauce

In medium skillet, add oil, sausage, and bell pepper. Over medium heat cook 5 minutes. Add pasta sauce. Cook until hot.

PULLED PORK ROAST

1 pound boneless pork roast, browned

1 (10¾ ounce) can French onion soup

2 tablespoons ketchup

1 tablespoon cider vinegar

1 tablespoon packed brown sugar

Sandwich rolls, split

In 1½-quart slow cooker, place roast. In medium bowl, combine remaining ingredients, except rolls. Mix well. Pour mixture over roast. Cover. Cook on low 6 to 8 hours. Shred pork. Put meat on rolls.

SALSA & CHILI PORK ROAST

1 pound pork roast

6 tablespoons thick n' chunky salsa

6 tablespoons chili sauce

⅛ teaspoon red pepper

1 tablespoon tomato paste

In 1½-quart slow cooker, place roast. In small bowl, combine salsa, chili, red pepper, and tomato paste. Mix well. Spoon mixture over roast. Cover. Cook on low 6 to 8 hours.

GLAZED PORK ROAST

¾ cup chicken broth
1 cup apricot preserves
1 teaspoon Dijon style mustard
1 small onion, chopped
1 pound boneless pork loin

In 1½-quart slow cooker, combine all ingredients, except pork. Mix well. Add pork. Cover. Cook on low 6 to 7 hours.

WEEKNIGHT PORK RIBS

1 pound boneless country style pork ribs
¼ teaspoon ground ginger
¼ cup teriyaki baste and glaze
2 tablespoons ketchup
2 tablespoons pineapple preserves

Coat 1½-quart slow cooker with cooking spray, place ribs. In small bowl, combine remaining ingredients. Mix well. Pour mixture over ribs. Cover. Cook on low 7 to 8 hours.

ADD SEVERAL DROPS OF OIL TO YOUR SKILLET
WHEN FRYING WITH BUTTER TO KEEP THE
BUTTER FROM BURNING.

ROSEMARY MARINATED PORK LOIN

¼ cup soy sauce
2 tablespoons water
1½ tablespoons brown sugar
½ teaspoon dried rosemary
2 boneless pork loin chops

Preheat oven to 350 degrees. In large resealable plastic bag, add soy sauce, water, brown sugar, and rosemary. Shake to mix. Add pork, shake to coat. Refrigerate at least 3 hours, turning once half way through. Drain, discard marinade. Place chops in greased baking dish. Bake 30 to 35 minutes.

SOUTHWESTERN GRILLED PORK

½ cup mayonnaise
1 tablespoon lime juice
1 clove garlic, minced
½ teaspoon chipotle chili powder
2 pork chops

In small bowl, combine all ingredients, except pork. Mix well. Divide sauce in half. Grill chops, basting frequently half way through cooking. Serve with reserved sauce.

PORK CHOPS & APPLES

1 (10¾ ounce) can mushroom soup
¼ cup water
1 teaspoon packed brown sugar
½ teaspoon Worcestershire sauce
2 (¾-inch thick) pork chops
1 apple, sliced
1 small onion, sliced

In 3-quart slow cooker, combine soup, water, brown sugar, and Worcestershire sauce. Mix well. Add pork chops. Top with apples and onions. Cover. Cook on low 6 to 8 hours.

PORK CHOPS IN TOMATOES

2 (1-inch thick) pork loin chops, browned
½ cup chopped tomatoes
½ cup sliced celery
1 cup pasta sauce

In 1½-quart slow cooker, place chops. In medium bowl, combine remaining ingredients. Mix well. Pour mixture over chops. Cover. Cook on low 6 to 7 hours.

HOT HONEY CHOPS

1½ tablespoons hot pepper sauce
3 tablespoons honey
2 (1-inch thick) pork chops

In small bowl, combine hot sauce and honey. Mix well. Place chops on grill. Cook over medium heat 3 minutes on both sides. Baste with mixture. Cook 6 minutes on both sides.

BREADED PORK CHOPS

2 eggs beaten
½ teaspoon salt
2 or 4 thin pork chops
1 cup crushed crackers
2 tablespoons oil
⅓ cup water

In shallow dish, combine eggs and salt. Dip chops in egg mixture. Pour cracker crumbs on plate. Press chops in crackers on both sides. In medium skillet with oil, brown chops over medium high heat. Add water, steam 3 minutes.

SIMPLE SALSA PORK CHOPS

2 pork loin chops
1 teaspoon salt
½ teaspoon pepper
1 cup salsa

Season chops with salt and pepper, place in medium skillet with oil. Over high heat brown both sides. Reduce heat to low. Add salsa. Cover. Simmer 8 minutes.

WHEN USING BAMBOO SKEWERS, SOAK THEM
IN WATER FOR ABOUT AN HOUR BEFORE
GRILLING TO PREVENT THEM FROM BURNING.

BARBEQUE PORK SKILLET

2 pork loin chops
2 tablespoons Italian dressing
2 tablespoons barbeque sauce
½ teaspoon chili powder

In medium skillet, brown pork chops over medium heat. In small bowl, combine remaining ingredients. Mix well. Spread mixture over chops. Cover. Cook on low 6 to 8 minutes.

BAKED HAM

½ pound ham
½ cup honey
1 tablespoon orange juice
⅛ teaspoon ground cloves
⅛ teaspoon cinnamon

Preheat oven to 325 degrees. In baking dish, place ham, bake 30 minutes. In small bowl, combine remaining ingredients. Mix well. Divide sauce, saving half for serving. Baste ham. Bake 20 minutes, basting 2 more times.

HAM & PINEAPPLE KABOBS

½ pound cooked ham, cut in 1-inch cubes
1 (8 ounce) can pineapple chunks, drained
1 medium green bell pepper, cut into chunks
⅓ cup barbecue sauce
¼ cup orange marmalade

Use 4 (10-inch) wooden skewers. Thread ham, pineapple, and bell pepper. In small bowl, combine sauce and marmalade. Mix well. Brush mixture over kabobs. Grill over medium heat 3 to 4 minutes.

HAM WITH PEACHES

1 pound fully cooked ham slice
1 cup diced peaches
2 tablespoons packed brown sugar
⅛ teaspoon cinnamon
1½ teaspoons butter

In medium skillet, brown ham over medium heat. Cover ham with peaches. Sprinkle brown sugar and cinnamon over top. Dot with butter. Cover. Cook 2 to 3 minutes or until sugar and butter has melted.

IT'S CHICKEN NIGHT

1 (10¾ ounce) can cream of chicken soup
⅓ cup water
1 large carrot, sliced
2 boneless, skinless, chicken breasts

In 1½-quart slow cooker, combine all ingredients, except chicken. Mix well. Add chicken, turn to coat. Cover. Cook on low 6 to 8 hours.

CHICKEN CACCIATORE

¾ cup chicken broth
¼ teaspoon garlic powder
1 (14½ ounce) can diced Italian style tomatoes
1 small onion, chopped
1 pound chicken parts, skin removed

In 1½-quart slow cooker, combine all ingredients, except chicken. Mix well. Add chicken, turn to coat. Cover. Cook on low 6 to 8 hours. Serve over spaghetti.

CHICKEN THIGHS IN SAUCE

4 skinless chicken thighs

1½ cups pasta sauce

⅛ teaspoon crushed red pepper

¼ cup half-and-half

2 cups hot cooked penne pasta

In 3-quart slow cooker, place chicken thighs. In medium bowl, combine pasta sauce and red pepper. Mix well. Pour mixture over chicken. Cover. Cook on low 6 to 7 hours. Add half-and-half. Spoon sauce over hot pasta.

BAKED CHICKEN STRIPS

2 tablespoons butter or margarine, melted

¾ cup crushed Rice Krispies® cereal

1 tablespoon flour

1 teaspoon seasoned salt

½ pound boneless, skinless chicken breasts strips

Preheat oven to 400 degrees. In small bowl, place butter. In medium bowl, combine cereal, flour, and salt. Mix well. Dip chicken in butter; roll in cereal mixture, pressing to coat. Place on lightly greased 9 x 13-inch baking dish. Drizzle remaining butter over chicken. Bake 25 to 30 minutes.

SOS SOAP PADS (SAVE OUR SAUCEPANS)
WERE INVENTED BY ALUMINUM POT
SALESMAN, ED COX , OF SAN FRANCISCO
IN 1917.

NACHO CHEESE CHICKEN STRIPS

2 eggs

2 tablespoons milk

2 boneless, skinless, chicken breasts, cut in strips

2 cups finely crushed nacho cheese tortilla chips

Preheat oven to 400 degrees. In small bowl, combine eggs and milk. Mix well. Dip chicken in egg mixture, roll in chips, place on greased baking sheet. Bake 15 minutes. Turn, bake 15 minutes or until golden brown.

BAKED BBQ CHICKEN

1 cup barbecue sauce

¼ cup diced onion

2 boneless, skinless, chicken breasts

Preheat oven 350 degrees. In small bowl, combine barbecue sauce and onion. Coat chicken with sauce. Place in 9 x 9-inch baking dish. Cover. Bake 30 minutes. Uncover, bake 10 minutes or until fully cooked

WHEN PREPARING STUFFING FOR A
TURKEY, ALLOW ONE CUP OF STUFFING
FOR EACH POUND OF MEAT.

BAKED CHICKEN PARMESAN

2 boneless, skinless, chicken breast halves
1 egg, beaten
½ cup Italian seasoned bread crumbs
1½ cups pasta sauce
½ cup shredded mozzarella cheese

Preheat oven to 400 degrees. Dip chicken in egg, then in bread crumbs. In 2-quart baking dish, place chicken. Bake 20 minutes. Pour pasta sauce over chicken, top with cheese. Bake 10 to 15 minutes or until cheese melts.

DELICIOUS FRIED CHICKEN

1 teaspoon garlic salt
½ teaspoon pepper
2 boneless chicken breasts
⅓ cup flour
1 tablespoon margarine
2 tablespoons oil

Salt and pepper chicken. Dredge chicken in flour. In medium skillet, add margarine and oil. Heat over medium heat until hot. Add chicken. Brown on both sides. Reduce heat to low. Cover. Cook 10 to 15 minutes.

IS IT FRIED CHICKEN

½ cup dry breadcrumbs

½ teaspoon seasoned salt

½ cup buttermilk

2 boneless, skinless, chicken breasts

Preheat oven to 400 degrees. In small bowl, combine breadcrumbs and seasoned salt. Pour buttermilk in shallow dish. Dip chicken in buttermilk then crumb mixture. Coat 2-quart baking dish with cooking spray. Add chicken. Bake 35 to 40 minutes.

HONEY MUSTARD CHICKEN

3 teaspoons Dijon mustard

2 teaspoons apricot jam

1 tablespoon honey

2 boneless, skinless, chicken breasts

Preheat oven to 350 degrees. In small bowl, combine mustard, honey, and jam. Mix well. Coat chicken breast with mustard mixture. Place in 9 x 9-inch baking dish. Pour remaining mustard mixture over chicken. Cover. Bake 30 minutes. Uncover, bake 10 minutes or until fully cooked.

WHEN CUTTING RAW POULTRY, USE A
PLASTIC CUTTING BOARD. IT IS EASIER
TO CLEAN AND DISINFECT THAN A
WOODEN ONE.

ORANGE GLAZED CHICKEN

½ cup orange juice

2 tablespoons brown sugar

2 teaspoons Dijon mustard

2 boneless, skinless, chicken breasts

Preheat oven to 350 degrees. In small bowl, combine orange juice, mustard, and brown sugar. Mix well. Coat chicken with orange sauce. Place in greased 9 x 9-inch baking pan. Pour remaining sauce over top. Cover. Bake 30 minutes. Uncover, bake 10 minutes or until fully cooked.

APPLESAUCE CHICKEN

2 boneless, skinless, chicken breasts

1 teaspoon butter or margarine

½ apple, sliced thin

½ cup applesauce

Preheat oven to 350 degrees. In large skillet, brown chicken in butter over medium heat. Place chicken in greased 9 x 9-inch baking dish. Top with apple slices and applesauce. Cover. Bake 20 minutes. Uncover, bake 10 minutes.

CORDON BLEU CHICKEN

2 boneless, skinless, chicken breasts
1 tablespoon butter or margarine
½ cup chicken broth
2 tablespoons balsamic vinegar
2 deli ham slices
2 slices mozzarella cheese

In medium skillet, brown chicken in butter over medium heat until fully cooked. Reduce heat, add broth and vinegar. Simmer 3 minutes. Drain liquid. Top each breast with ham and cheese. Cover until cheese has melted.

THAI CHICKEN

6 tablespoons unsweetened coconut milk
2 tablespoons creamy peanut butter
⅛ teaspoon ground garlic
2 boneless, skinless, chicken breasts
½ tablespoon vegetable oil
2 green onions, cut into 1-inch pieces, including tops

In small bowl, combine milk, peanut butter, and garlic. Mix well, set aside. In large medium skillet, brown chicken in oil until fully cooked, over medium heat. Remove chicken from skillet, keep warm. Add green onions to skillet, cook 3 minutes. Add peanut mixture, cook and stir until bubbly. Pour sauce over chicken. Serve with rice if desired.

ASIAN CHICKEN

⅓ cup soy sauce

2 tablespoons orange juice

1 tablespoon lime juice

1 clove garlic, minced

2 boneless, skinless, chicken breasts

In large resealable plastic bag. Combine all ingredients. Shake to mix. Marinate 20 minutes, turning after 10 minutes. Discard marinade. Grill or broil chicken until fully cooked.

TERIYAKI CHICKEN

¼ cup chicken broth

¼ cup brown sugar

½ tablespoon soy sauce

1 clove garlic, minced

2 boneless, skinless, chicken breasts, cubed

In large skillet, combine all ingredients. Over medium heat cook until chicken is fully cooked. Serve with rice if desired.

SPICY RUBBED CHICKEN

1 teaspoon garlic powder

½ teaspoon chili powder

¼ teaspoon paprika

¼ teaspoon salt

2 boneless, skinless, chicken breasts

In small bowl, combine all spices. Mix well. Rub spices on all sides of chicken. In medium skillet, spray cooking spray. Over medium heat cook chicken until fully cooked.

MEDITERRANEAN CHICKEN

2 boneless, skinless, chicken breasts
2 tablespoons olive oil
½ onion, diced
1 tomato, seeded, chopped
¼ cup sliced green olives
2 tablespoons red wine vinegar

In large skillet, brown chicken in olive oil over medium heat. Add onion halfway through browning. Reduce heat to low. Add remaining ingredients. Cover. Cook 10 minutes.

SALSA CHICKEN

2 boneless, skinless, chicken breasts
½ cup salsa
½ cup shredded cheddar cheese

Preheat oven to 350 degrees. In large skillet, brown chicken over medium heat. Remove, place in 9 x 9-inch baking dish. Pour salsa into skillet. Over low heat, stir salsa for 1 minute, pour over chicken. Sprinkle cheese over each chicken breast. Bake 10 minutes.

**NEVER USE THE SAME PLATE FOR
UNCOOKED AND COOKED POULTRY.**

TACO CHICKEN

2 boneless, skinless, chicken breasts, cubed
1½ tablespoons taco seasoning
1 tablespoon vegetable oil
1½ cups chunky salsa
¼ cup peach preserves

Sprinkle taco seasoning on chicken. In large skillet, brown chicken in oil over medium heat. In small bowl, combine salsa and preserves. Mix well. Add to skillet, bring to boil. Reduce heat to low. Cover. Simmer 3 to 4 minutes. Serve with rice if desired.

JALAPENO SAUCE CHICKEN

2 boneless, skinless, chicken breasts
2 tablespoons butter or margarine
1 cup chopped celery
2 tablespoons water
¼ cup jalapeno jelly
½ tablespoon Dijon mustard

In large skillet, brown chicken in butter over medium high heat, until fully cooked. Remove, set aside. In same skillet, add water, scraping up crusty pieces. Add celery. Cook 2 minutes. Add jelly, mustard, and chicken. Cook 4 minutes.

FRENCH CHICKEN

1 cup thinly sliced onion
3 tablespoons French dressing
2 boneless, skinless, chicken breasts

Preheat oven to 350 degrees. In 9 x 9-inch baking dish, place onion. Coat chicken with dressing, place over onions. Drizzle remaining dressing over top. Cover. Bake 30 minutes. Uncover. Bake 10 minutes.

RASPBERRY GLAZED CHICKEN

2 tablespoons raspberry preserves
2 tablespoons water
1 tablespoon plus 1 teaspoon white wine vinegar
1½ teaspoons grill seasoning for chicken
½ teaspoon cornstarch
2 boneless, skinless, chicken breasts

Preheat oven to 350 degrees. In small saucepan, combine all ingredients except chicken, mix well. Over medium high heat, bring to a boil. Cook until thickens. Place chicken in 9 x 9-inch baking dish. Pour ½ of raspberry mixture over chicken. Cover with foil. Bake 30 minutes. Pour remaining raspberry mixture over chicken. Bake uncovered 20 minutes.

**SINCE 1868 TABASCO SAUCE HAS
BEEN ADDING SPICE TO FOODS.**

SOUTHERN STYLE PECAN CHICKEN

2 boneless, skinless, chicken breasts, pounded to ¼-inch thick

2 tablespoons Dijon mustard

2 tablespoons honey

½ cup finely chopped pecans

Preheat oven to 350 degrees. Grease13 x 9 x 2-inch baking dish. In small bowl, combine mustard and honey. Mix well. Spread chicken with mustard mixture, roll in pecans, place in dish. Bake 30 minutes.

SCALED DOWN CHICKEN BAKE

2 boneless, skinless, chicken breasts, browned

1 (10¾ ounce) can mushroom soup

¼ cup sliced mushrooms

½ cup milk

Preheat oven to 350 degrees. In 2 quart baking dish, place chicken. In medium bowl, combine remaining ingredients. Mix well. Pour mixture over chicken. Cover. Bake 50 to 60 minutes.

BREADED CHICKEN BREAST

¼ cup mayonnaise

2 tablespoons grated parmesan cheese

2 boneless, skinless, chicken breasts

¼ cup Italian seasoned dry bread crumbs

Preheat oven to 425 degrees. In small bowl, combine mayonnaise and parmesan cheese. Mix well. Dip chicken in mixture. Dredge in bread crumbs. Place on baking sheet. Bake 30 minutes or until fully cooked.

RANCH CHICKEN

¼ cup bread crumbs

1 (1 ounce) packet Ranch style salad dressing mix

2 boneless, skinless, chicken breasts

Preheat oven to 375 degrees. In small bowl, combine crumbs and Ranch mix. Mix well. Dredge chicken in crumb mixture, place on ungreased baking sheet. Bake 40 to 50 minutes.

LEMON CHICKEN

2 boneless, skinless, chicken breasts

3 tablespoons lemon juice

¼ cup butter, melted

½ teaspoon poultry seasoning

½ teaspoon garlic salt

Preheat oven to 350 degrees. In greased 9 x 9-inch baking dish, place chicken. In small bowl, combine remaining ingredients. Mix well. Pour over chicken. Cover. Bake 30 minutes. Uncover. Bake 10 minutes, baste often. Serve with rice.

SLOW COOKER CORNISH HENS

2 Cornish hens

2 tablespoons butter or margarine

½ cup chicken broth

Salt & lemon pepper to taste

In large skillet, brown chicken in butter over medium high heat. Place chicken in slow cooker. Add chicken broth. Sprinkle with salt and pepper if desired. Cover. Cook on low 7 to 9 hours.

GRILLED CORNISH HEN

⅓ cup soy sauce

2 tablespoons packed brown sugar

1 clove garlic, minced

Cornish hen, cut in half

In medium bowl, combine all ingredients, except hen. Mix well. Place hen in mixture. Coat well. Cover. Refrigerate 4 hours. Place hen halves on grill. Cook over medium heat 40 minutes, turning often.

SHRIMP KABOBS

¼ cup chili sauce

½ tablespoon honey

¼ pound large shrimp, peeled, deveined

¼ pound kielbasa, sliced into 1-inch pieces

1 small green bell pepper, cut into chunks

In small bowl, combine chili sauce and honey. Mix well. On skewers, thread shrimp, sausage, and pepper, repeat. Brush kabobs with sauce. Place on grill, over medium heat, until shrimp is cooked, brushing frequently with sauce.

HENRY FORD INVENTED THE CHARCOAL BRIQUETTE WITH THE HELP OF THOMAS EDISON IN 1920.

CHILI SPICED SHRIMP

    1 pound shrimp, shelled, deveined
    2 tablespoons butter or margarine
    1 teaspoon lime juice
    ¾ teaspoon chili powder
    ¼ teaspoon garlic salt

In large skillet, combine all ingredients. Over medium high heat cook 8 to 10 minutes or until shrimp is cooked.

PIZZAZZ SHRIMP

    1 tablespoon olive oil
    ⅛ teaspoon red pepper
    ½ pound uncooked shrimp, peeled, deveined
    1½ cups pasta sauce

In medium skillet, add oil, red pepper, and shrimp. Over medium high heat cook 3 minutes. Add pasta sauce. Simmer 5 minutes or until shrimp is pink.

HONEY MUSTARD SALMON

    ¼ cup honey mustard marinade
    1 teaspoon lemon juice
    ¼ teaspoon garlic pepper
    2 (4 to 6 ounce) salmon steaks

In small bowl, combine mustard, lemon juice, and pepper. Mix well. Place salmon on grill. Over medium heat cook 10 to 15 minutes or until fish flakes. Baste with mustard mixture frequently during the last 5 minutes.

GRILLED SALMON

¼ cup olive oil

2 tablespoons plus 2 teaspoons molasses

1 clove garlic, minced

¾ teaspoon grated lemon peel

2 (6 ounce) salmon fillets

In small bowl, combine all ingredients, except salmon. Mix well. Divide sauce, saving half for serving. Spray grill with cooking spray. Cook over medium heat. Cook 8 to 10 minutes on each side, baste as it cooks.

CRUSTED BAKED SALMON

1 pound salmon fillet

2 tablespoons mayonnaise

1 teaspoon Dijon mustard

¼ cup croutons, crushed

⅓ cup chopped pecans

Preheat oven to 350 degrees. In 2-quart baking dish, place salmon. In small bowl, combine mayonnaise and mustard. Mix well. Coat salmon with mixture. Sprinkle croutons and pecans over top. Bake 20 to 30 minutes or until salmon flakes. Can grill over medium heat.

C STANDS FOR COOKED. BOILED OR
STEAMED SHRIMP WILL FORM A LETTER "C"
WHEN IT IS COOKED.

O STANDS FOR OVERCOOKED. WHEN SHRIMP
IS OVERCOOKED IT WILL FORM A LETTER "O".

ORIENTAL FISH FILLETS

2 (6 ounce) cod fillets
1 teaspoon fresh grated ginger
1 green onion, chopped with tops
1 tablespoon soy sauce
1 tablespoon rice vinegar

Preheat oven to 425 degrees. Prepare 2 large pieces of aluminum foil. Place fillets on foil, bring edges up around fish. Spread each fillet with ginger. Top with onion. In small bowl mix soy sauce and vinegar. Mix well. Drizzle sauce over fillets. Close foil around fish, sealing well, place on baking sheet. Bake 10 minutes or until fish flakes.

BAKED FISH FILLETS

1 pound fish fillets
½ teaspoon salt
½ cup tartar sauce
½ cup French fried onions

Preheat oven to 350 degrees. Cut fish into serving size pieces. Layer fish in 2-quart baking dish. Bake 30 minutes. Remove from oven. Spread tartar sauce over fish. Top with onions. Bake 3 minutes or until onions are crisp.

MARINATE MEAT IN A HEAVY-DUTY
ZIP LOCK PLASTIC BAG FOR EASY
CLEAN UP.

TUNA STEAK BURGERS

½ pound tuna steak, chopped
1 tablespoon soy sauce
½ teaspoon grated fresh ginger
⅛ teaspoon pepper
2 tablespoons bread crumbs
1 tablespoon sesame seeds

In small bowl, combine tuna, soy sauce, ginger, and pepper. Mix well. Shape 2 patties. In small bowl, combine crumbs and seeds. Mix well. Press patties into mixture, coating both sides. Spray grill or skillet with cooking spray. Grill or fry tuna to desired doneness.

ITALIAN TUNA STEAKS

2 (6 to 8 ounce) tuna steaks
1 (8 ounce) bottle Italian dressing
½ cup salsa

In small bowl, place tuna. Pour Italian dressing over tuna. Cover. Marinate 1 hour. Grill over medium heat 15 to 20 minutes or until tuna flakes. Top with salsa.

FRIED CATFISH

¼ cup flour

¼ cup cornmeal

½ teaspoon salt

1 egg

¼ cup milk

2 whole or fillet catfish

Oil

In shallow pan, combine flour, cornmeal, and salt. Mix well. In shallow bowl, beat egg and milk. Dip fish in egg mixture, then in dry mixture. Coat well. Place in medium skillet with hot oil. Over medium heat fry until golden brown or until fish flakes.

PRETZEL COATED CATFISH

2 (4 ounce) catfish fillets

1 egg, beaten

1½ tablespoons Dijon mustard

½ tablespoon milk

2 tablespoons flour

½ cup crushed pretzels

2 tablespoons vegetable oil

In small bowl, combine mustard, milk, and flour. Mix well. In small bowl, place flour. In small bowl, place pretzels. Coat fish with flour. Dip in egg mixture. Dredge in pretzel. In medium skillet, brown fish in oil, over medium heat, until golden brown and flaky.

CATFISH FRY

2 catfish fillets

1 cup buttermilk

½ cup yellow cornmeal

1 teaspoon Cajun seasoning

¼ cup vegetable oil

Marinate catfish in buttermilk for 30 minutes. In small bowl, combine cornmeal and seasoning. Mix well. In medium skillet, over medium high heat, heat oil. Dredge fish in cornmeal. Place in hot oil. Fry until golden brown.

HALIBUT STEAKS

2 halibut steaks

1 tablespoon butter or margarine

1 tablespoon lemon juice

Preheat oven to 400 degrees. Place halibut in small baking dish. In small bowl, combine butter and lemon juice. Spread mixture over halibut. Bake 20 minutes or until fish flakes.

LEMON PEPPER HALIBUT

1½ tablespoons butter or margarine

2 halibut fillets

¾ teaspoon lemon pepper seasoning

1 small onion, sliced

In medium skillet, melt butter over medium high heat. Sprinkle halibut with lemon pepper. Add to skillet. Top with onions. Cook 5 to 8 minutes or until halibut is white and no longer opaque.

TARTAR SAUCE FOR FISH

½ cup mayonnaise

¼ cup sweet pickle relish, drained

1 teaspoon lemon juice

In small bowl, combine all ingredients. Mix well. Chill. Makes ¾ cup.

EMERGENCY BBQ SAUCE

½ cup ketchup

3 tablespoons packed brown sugar

1 teaspoon sugar

2 tablespoons maple syrup

¼ teaspoon liquid smoke

In small saucepan, combine all ingredients. Mix well. Over low heat, simmer 15 minutes. Makes ½ cup.

A SAUCE FOR BEEF

½ cup sour cream

1 tablespoon cream style horseradish

1 teaspoon mayonnaise

½ teaspoon sugar

In small bowl, combine all ingredients. Mix well. Serve with beef. Makes over ½ cup.

SPICE IT UP PORK RUB

> 1 tablespoon chili powder
> 1 teaspoon ground cumin
> ¼ teaspoon salt
> 1 large clove garlic, diced

In small bowl, combine all ingredients. Mix well. Rub evenly on both sides of pork roast or chops before grilling.

ORANGE BUTTER FOR LAMB CHOPS

> 2 tablespoons butter, softened
> 1 tablespoon orange marmalade
> ¼ teaspoon dried marjoram leaves

In small bowl, combine all ingredients. Mix well. Serve over cooked lamb.

**BY 1975 SALES OF MICROWAVE OVENS
EXCEEDED SALES OF GAS RANGES.**

NOTES

Vegetables

ROASTED ASPARAGUS

½ pound asparagus, trimmed

2 teaspoons olive oil

⅛ teaspoon salt

Preheat oven to 450 degrees. In medium bowl, combine all ingredients. Toss well. Arrange asparagus in single layer on cookie sheet. Cook until partly browned and tips are beginning to crisp.

TABLE TOP GRILLED ASPARAGUS

8 fresh asparagus spears, trimmed

1 small red bell pepper, cut into strips

2 tablespoons Italian dressing

2 tablespoons shredded parmesan cheese

Heat contact grill 5 minutes. In medium bowl, combine all ingredients, except cheese. Mix well. When grill is heated, place half of vegetables crosswise on bottom grill surface. Close grill. Cook 4 to 5 minutes or until vegetables are crisp tender. Place in serving bowl. Repeat with remaining vegetables. Sprinkle with cheese

ITALIAN STYLE ASPARAGUS

½ pound fresh asparagus spears, trimmed

1 tablespoon olive oil

¼ teaspoon garlic salt

Preheat oven to broil. On baking sheet, place asparagus. Drizzle with olive oil. Sprinkle garlic salt over asparagus. Toss to coat. Broil 5 minutes or until slightly browned. Turn, broil 3 minutes.

ASPARAGUS AU GRATIN

½ cup water
¾ pound fresh asparagus spears, trimmed
1 tablespoon Dijon mustard
¼ cup seasoned bread crumbs
¼ cup shredded Swiss cheese
1 tablespoon butter or margarine, melted

Preheat oven to 400 degrees. In medium saucepan, add water, over medium high heat bring to boil. Add asparagus, cook 4 minutes, drain. Add mustard. Mix well. In small bowl combine remaining ingredients. Mix well. Add half to asparagus. Mix well. In 9 x 9-inch baking ban, place asparagus. Top with remaining bread crumb mixture. Bake 20 minutes or until crumb mixture is golden brown.

SKILLET GREEN BEANS

½ pound fresh green beans, trimmed
1 tablespoon butter or margarine
salt & pepper

In large skillet, add water to ½ inch depth. Add green beans. Over medium high heat bring to a boil. Reduce heat to low. Cover. Cook 5 minutes or until tender. Drain. Add butter and salt and pepper to taste. Mix well.

ALMOST FRIED GREEN BEANS

1 teaspoon butter
½ teaspoon olive oil
½ teaspoon salt
2 tablespoons sliced almonds
½ pound green beans, cooked

In medium skillet, combine all ingredients, except green beans. Over medium heat cook 1 minute. Add green beans. Cook until hot.

NOW THAT'S GREEN BEANS

½ teaspoon butter or margarine
1 tablespoon diced onion
1 small garlic clove, minced
1 cup green beans
1 tablespoon shredded cheddar cheese

In small skillet, melt butter over medium heat. Add onion and garlic. Cook, stirring until onions begin to brown. Add green beans. Cook until hot. Add cheese and toss.

GREEN BEANS & TOASTED PECANS

3 cups water
½ pound fresh green beans, trimmed
2 tablespoons chopped pecans
1 tablespoon butter or margarine

In medium saucepan, bring water to a boil over medium high heat. Add green beans. Cook 10 minutes. Drain. In large skillet, sauté pecans in butter over medium high heat until golden. Add beans, toss to mix.

SPICED UP BEETS

>1 tablespoon chopped onions
>½ tablespoon butter
>1½ tablespoons honey
>1 tablespoon wine vinegar
>1 cup canned sliced beets, drained

In medium skillet, sauté onion in butter over medium heat until softened. Add honey and vinegar. Cook and stir until mixture begins to boil. Add beets. Cook until hot.

CITRUS FLAVOR BROCCOLI

>1½ cups fresh broccoli florets
>2 teaspoons butter
>1½ teaspoons flour
>½ cup orange juice

In medium saucepan, place broccoli in 1-inch of water. Over medium heat bring to a boil. Reduce heat to low. Simmer until crisp tender. Drain. In small saucepan, melt butter over medium heat. Add flour. Stir until smooth. Gradually stir in orange juice. Cook mixture until thickened. Add mixture to broccoli. Toss well.

YOU'VE GOTTA BE NUTS BRUSSELS SPROUTS

>½ pound Brussels sprouts, halved
>1 cup pecan halves
>2 tablespoons butter or margarine
>¼ teaspoon salt
>⅛ teaspoon pepper

In large skillet, combine all ingredients, sauté over medium heat for 6 to 8 minutes or until tender.

CLASSY ORANGE CARROTS

2 tablespoons orange marmalade

1 tablespoon butter or margarine

2 teaspoons orange flavor liqueur

1 cup frozen cut carrots, cooked

In small saucepan, combine marmalade, butter, and liqueur. Mix well. Over medium heat cook until hot. Add carrots. Reduce heat to low. Cook 2 minutes.

CAULIFLOWER AU GRATIN

2 cups frozen cauliflower florets, thawed

½ cup cubed Velveeta®

6 tablespoons shredded cheddar cheese

½ cup crushed corn flakes

Preheat oven to 375 degrees. In 1-quart baking dish, microwave cauliflower for 3 minutes. Drain. Top with cheeses. Sprinkle with corn flakes. Bake 10 to 12 minutes or until golden brown.

CREAMED CORN

1 slice bacon

2 ears corn, remove kernels

2 tablespoons finely chopped red bell pepper

2 tablespoons milk

¼ cup cream cheese with onion and chives, softened

In medium skillet brown bacon over medium heat. Drain. Add corn, pepper, and milk to skillet. Over medium heat cook 8 minutes or until corn is tender. Add cream cheese and crumble bacon into pan. Cook 3 minutes.

GRILLED CORN

>2 tablespoons butter or margarine, softened
>½ teaspoon lemon pepper
>2 ears fresh corn

In small bowl, combine butter and lemon pepper. Mix well. Spread mixture on corn, wrap in aluminum foil. Grill corn for 20 minutes over medium heat, turning halfway through.

CORN STUFFED PEPPERS

>1 red bell pepper, cut lengthwise, seeded
>1 cup canned corn, drained
>½ teaspoon butter or margarine, melted
>salt and pepper

Preheat oven to 350 degrees. Place peppers cut side up on baking sheet. In small bowl, combine corn, butter, and salt and pepper to taste. Mix well. Fill peppers with corn. Bake 20 to 25 minutes.

IT'S A SNAP PEAS

>½ pound sugar snap peas, trimmed
>1 teaspoon butter or margarine
>½ teaspoon salt

In large saucepan, cook peas in boiling water 2 minutes. Drain. Add butter and salt. Mix well.

ZESTY SNAP PEAS

1 tablespoon butter or margarine

½ pound sugar snap peas, trimmed

½ teaspoon grated lemon zest

¼ teaspoon dried thyme

In large skillet, melt butter over medium high heat. Add peas. Cook 2 minutes. Add zest and thyme. Cook 1 minute.

GREEN PEPPER BAKE

½ cup balsamic vinegar

1 green bell pepper, sliced in ½-inch strips

1 tablespoon olive oil

Preheat oven 450 degrees. In small saucepan, reduce balsamic vinegar by half over medium high heat. Place peppers in 9 x 9- inch baking dish. Drizzle olive oil over peppers, toss to coat. Bake 15 minutes or until browned. Drizzle vinegar over top, toss to coat.

SPUDS & MORE

1½ cups frozen vegetables

1 (10¾ ounce) can cream of broccoli soup

⅓ cup shredded cheddar cheese

2 large baking potatoes, baked

In medium saucepan, combine all ingredients, except potatoes. Over medium heat cook until hot. Mix well. Split potatoes. Pour mixture over top.

HOME SWEET HOME FRIES

2 medium russet potatoes, cubed
1½ teaspoons butter or margarine
salt and pepper to taste

In medium skillet, combine all ingredients. Cover. Over medium high heat cook 10 minutes. Remove lid. Cook until golden.

ALMOST FRIED POTATOES

2 cups sliced potatoes
2 tablespoons Ranch dressing
⅛ teaspoon black pepper

Heat contact grill 5 minutes. In medium bowl, combine all ingredients. Mix well. When grill is heated, place potatoes evenly on bottom grill surface. Close grill. Cook 15 to 20 minutes, turning potatoes 2 or 3 times until potatoes are fork tender.

PARSLEY POTATOES

1 pound red new potatoes, halved
1 tablespoon salted butter, melted
1 tablespoon chopped parsley
2 tablespoons chopped chives

In medium saucepan, add potatoes, cover with water. Over medium high heat cook until tender. Drain. Place in bowl. Add remaining ingredients. Toss to coat.

GARLIC ROASTED POTATOES

1 pound Yukon gold potatoes with skins, cut into chunks

2 tablespoons olive oil

2 cloves garlic, minced

Salt and pepper

Preheat oven to 450 degrees. In medium saucepan, add potatoes, cover with water. Over medium high heat bring to a boil. Boil 2 minutes. Place potatoes in 13 x 9 x 2-inch baking pan. Drizzle potatoes with olive oil. Add garlic. Season with salt and pepper to taste. Toss to coat. Bake 20 minutes. Toss. Bake 10 minutes.

TWICE COOKED POTATOES

2 large russet potatoes

¼ cup sour cream

2 tablespoons butter

1 teaspoon milk

¼ cup shredded cheddar cheese

Preheat oven to 350 degrees. Prick potatoes with fork. Microwave for 10 minutes or until tender. Cut potato in half, scoop out pulp. In small bowl, combine pulp, sour cream, butter, and milk. Mix well. Spoon into potato skins. Top with cheese. Bake 15 minutes or until cheese has melted.

BEFORE COOKING CAULIFLOWER, SOAK FLOWERETS IN COLD WATER TO DRAW OUT HIDDEN INSECTS.

AU GRATIN POTATOES

2 large potatoes, sliced

1 (10¾ ounce) can cream of mushroom soup

¼ cup chopped onions

½ cup milk

½ cup shredded cheddar cheese

In 1½-quart slow cooker, combine all ingredients. Mix well. Cover. Cook on low 5 to 6 hours.

FIERY FRIES

½ tablespoon olive oil

¼ teaspoon seasoned salt

⅛ teaspoon Cajun seasoning

⅛ teaspoon chili seasoning

2 medium potatoes, cut into fries

Preheat oven to 375 degrees. Line baking sheet with foil, coat with cooking spray. In small bowl, combine oil and seasonings. Mix well. Place fries on baking sheet. Drizzle with seasoning mixture. Toss to coat. Bake 45 minutes or until golden brown, turning half way through baking.

CAJUN FRIES

2 large potatoes, cut into fries

1 egg white, beaten

1 tablespoon Cajun seasoning

Preheat oven to 400 degrees. Coat baking sheet with cooking spray. In medium bowl, combine all ingredients. Mix well. Arrange potatoes in single layer. Bake 40 minutes or until crisp.

PARMESAN FRENCH FRIES

¼ cup grated parmesan cheese

1 teaspoon dried oregano

2 medium potatoes, sliced into fries

1 egg white, beaten

Preheat oven to 425 degrees. In small bowl, combine cheese and oregano. Mix well. Dip potato in egg, roll in cheese, place on greased baking sheet. Bake 25 minutes or until golden brown.

CREAMY GARLIC MASHED POTATOES

2 large potatoes, peeled, diced

2 cloves garlic, minced

½ teaspoon salt

2 tablespoons heavy whipping cream

2 tablespoons butter or margarine

In large saucepan, add potatoes and garlic, cover with water. Over medium high heat bring to a boil. Reduce heat to low. Cover. Simmer 10 minutes or until tender. Drain. In medium bowl, mash potatoes and garlic. Add remaining ingredients. Mix well.

MASHED POTATO BAKE

1½ cups mashed potatoes
½ cup sour cream
2 tablespoons milk
⅓ cup French fried onions
½ cup shredded cheddar cheese

Preheat oven to 350 degrees. In medium bowl, combine potatoes, sour cream, and milk. Mix well. Pour mixture into 1 quart casserole. Bake 20 minutes. Sprinkle onions and cheese on top. Bake 3 minutes.

JAZZED UP
INSTANT MASHED POTATOES

2 servings, instant mashed potatoes, warm
2 tablespoons sour cream
½ tablespoon dried minced onion

In small bowl, combine all ingredients. Mix well. Microwave 30 seconds.

SCALLOPED POTATO CASSEROLE

2 cups sliced potatoes
½ cup diced onion
¼ cup diced ham
1 (10¾ ounce) can cheddar cheese soup
½ cup milk

Coat 1½-quart slow cooker with cooking spray. Layer potatoes and onion in cooker. In small bowl, combine ham, soup, and milk. Mix well. Pour mixture over potatoes and onions. Cover. Cook on low 6 to 7 hours.

SQUASH CIRCLES

1 pound acorn squash
1 tablespoon butter or margarine
¼ cup packed brown sugar

Preheat oven to 400 degrees. Slice tip and stem end from squash. Cut squash crosswise into ¾-inch rings. Scoop out and discard seeds. Place squash in baking pan. Dot butter and sprinkle brown sugar over squash. Cover. Bake 20 to 30 minutes or until squash is tender.

SWEET POTATO SPEARS

1 egg white
1 teaspoon chili powder
¼ teaspoon garlic salt
2 small sweet potatoes, peeled, sliced into ½-inch strips

Preheat oven 400 degrees. Coat baking sheet with cooking spray. In small bowl, combine egg, chili powder, and garlic salt. Mix well. Add potatoes. Toss to coat. Arrange in single layer on baking sheet. Bake 25 minutes or until golden brown.

GRILLED STUFFED SWEET POTATOES

1 large sweet potato
1 tablespoon butter
1 tablespoon orange marmalade
¼ teaspoon salt

Microwave potato until almost tender. Cut in half, scoop pulp into small bowl, leaving ¼-inch potato in each half. Mash potatoes. Stir in butter, marmalade, and salt. Spoon mixture into potato shells. Place on grill. Over medium heat cook 8 to 10 minutes.

CANDIED SWEET POTATOES

> 2 medium sweet potatoes
> 2 tablespoons butter
> 2½ tablespoons packed brown sugar
> 2 tablespoons water

Preheat oven to 350 degrees. In medium saucepan, place potatoes, cover with water. Cook over medium heat until tender. Peel and cut in half lengthwise. Place in 2-quart baking dish. In small bowl, combine remaining ingredients. Mix well. Spread mixture over potatoes. Cover. Bake 40 to 60 minutes.

BAKED TOMATO

> 1 tomato, cut in half
> 1 tablespoon Ranch dressing
> ⅛ teaspoon Italian seasoning

Preheat oven to 350 degrees. Place tomato halves, cut side up, on baking sheet. Bake 15 minutes. Spread dressing on top of tomato. Sprinkle with seasoning. Broil 3 inches from heat, 2 to 3 minutes.

MIXED VEGETABLE SAUTÉ

1 tablespoon butter or margarine

¼ pound fresh green beans, cut in 2-inch pieces

2 carrots, diced

¾ cup sliced mushrooms

½ teaspoon salt

In large skillet, melt butter over medium heat. Add all ingredients. Cook for 15 minutes or until tender.

DOUBLE CHEESY ZUCCHINI & SQUASH

1 small zucchini, sliced thin

1 small summer squash, sliced thin

1 cup shredded mozzarella cheese

¼ cup grated parmesan cheese

Preheat oven to 375 degrees. In greased 1-quart baking dish, layer zucchini and squash. Top with cheese. Bake 30 minutes or until cheese is golden brown.

MARINARA ZUCCHINI & SAUSAGE

1 zucchini, sliced

¼ cup chopped red bell pepper

2 Italian sausage links, browned, drained

½ cup marinara sauce

¼ cup shredded parmesan cheese

In medium saucepan, combine all ingredients. Mix well. Cover. Cook over medium low heat 15 to 20 minutes.

YUMMY YAMS

2 medium yams
2 tablespoons butter or margarine, softened
½ teaspoon powdered sugar
⅛ teaspoon cinnamon

Preheat oven to 425 degrees. Prick yams with fork. Bake 1 hour or until tender. In small bowl, combine remaining ingredients. Mix well. Cut slit in yams. Top with butter mixture.

FRIED RICE

2 cups cooked rice
1 cup diced frozen mixed vegetables
2 eggs
2 tablespoons balsamic vinaigrette salad dressing
2 tablespoons soy sauce

In large saucepan, add rice and vegetables. Over medium heat cook until warm. Add remaining ingredients. Mix well. Cook until eggs are fully cooked.

TO EXTEND THE LIFE OF FRESH PARSLEY, PLACE IT IN A GLASS JAR WITH A SMALL AMOUNT OF WATER. COVER THE JAR TIGHTLY, REFRIGERATE, AND CHANGE WATER EVERY FIVE DAYS.

CAJUN RICE

    2 tablespoons butter or margarine

    ½ teaspoon Cajun seasoning

    1 cup cooked rice

In small saucepan, melt butter over medium heat. Add seasoning, cook 2 minutes. Add rice. Mix well. Cook until heated.

WHITE SAUCE MAKES IT SPECIAL

    2 tablespoons butter

    2 tablespoons all-purpose flour

    ¼ teaspoon salt

    ½ cup shredded cheese

    1 cup milk

In small saucepan, melt butter over medium heat. Stir in flour and salt. Add milk, stirring constantly until sauce is thick. Add cheese. Mix well. Serve over cooked vegetables.

Breads

DOUBLE BUTTER BREAD

2 cups self-rising flour
⅓ cup sugar
1 teaspoon salt
1½ cups milk
½ cup peanut butter

Preheat oven to 375 degrees. In large bowl, combine flour, sugar, and salt. Mix well. Add milk and peanut butter. Blend well. Pour into greased loaf pan. Bake 40 to 50 minutes.

1-2-3 HOMEMADE BREAD

3 cups self-rising flour
3 tablespoons sugar
1 (12 ounce) can warm beer

Preheat oven to 350 degrees. In large bowl, add flour. Make a well in center of flour. Stir in remaining ingredients. Blend well. Pour in greased bread pan. Bake 40 to 45 minutes or until golden brown. Makes 1 loaf.

LEFTOVER BANANA BREAD

3 ripe bananas, mashed
2 eggs, well beaten
2 cups flour
¾ cup sugar
1 teaspoon salt
1 teaspoon soda
½ cup chopped walnuts

Preheat oven to 350 degrees. Grease loaf pan. In large bowl, combine bananas and eggs. Stir in flour, sugar, salt, and soda. Add walnuts and blend. Pour mixture into loaf plan. Bake 1 hour. Makes 1 loaf.

GARLIC FRIED BREAD

1 small loaf French bread, sliced in 1-inch pieces
3 tablespoons butter, softened
1 teaspoon minced garlic

In small bowl, combine butter and garlic. Mix well. Spread mixture on both sides of bread. In medium skillet, fry bread over medium high heat until golden brown on both sides.

BAKED CHEESE BREAD

1 small loaf French bread
3 tablespoons butter or margarine
½ cup shredded cheddar cheese
2 tablespoons parmesan cheese

Preheat oven to 350 degrees. Cut bread lengthwise into halves. Place on baking sheet. Spread butter evenly over halves. Sprinkle cheddar cheese and parmesan cheese over top. Bake 5 to 10 minutes or until cheese melts.

CHOPPED CHILE CHEESE BREAD

¼ cup cheese spread

2 tablespoons canned chopped green chiles, drained

4 slices 1-inch thick French bread

Preheat oven to 350 degrees. In small bowl, combine cheese spread and green chiles. Mix well. Spread mixture over bread slices. Place on baking sheet. Bake 6 to 8 minutes or until cheese is hot and bubbly.

CAJUN GARLIC BREAD

¼ teaspoon garlic powder

⅛ teaspoon ground red pepper

⅛ teaspoon dried oregano

2 tablespoons butter, melted

1 small loaf French bread

Preheat oven to 350 degrees. In small bowl, combine all ingredients, except bread. Mix well. Cut bread lengthwise into halves. Drizzle butter mixture over cut sides of bread. Place together. Wrap in foil. Bake 10 minutes.

CHEESY GARLIC SOURDOUGH BREAD

2 (½-inch thick) slices sourdough bread, cut in half

½ tablespoon olive oil

½ teaspoon garlic salt

¼ cup mozzarella cheese

Preheat oven to 350. On bread, spread oil. Sprinkle with garlic salt and mozzarella. Bake 15 minutes or until cheese is melted.

DOUBLE CHEESE GARLIC BREAD

4 (½-inch thick) slices French bread
2 tablespoons butter or margarine, softened
½ teaspoon minced garlic
¼ cup shredded Swiss cheese
1 tablespoon grated parmesan cheese

Preheat oven to 400 degrees. Place bread on baking sheet. In small bowl, combine butter and garlic, mix well. Spread butter mixture on one side of bread. In small bowl, combine cheeses, mix well. Sprinkle on top of butter. Bake 10 to 15 minutes or until cheese is melted.

MUSTARD TOAST

1 French sub roll, split apart
1 tablespoon Dijon mustard
2 slices Monterey jack cheese

Preheat oven to broil. On baking sheet, place roll. Spread mustard on cut sides of roll, top with cheese. Broil until cheese has melted and is slightly golden brown.

RASCAL BISCUITS

2 cups Bisquick®
1 tablespoon sugar
½ (12 ounce) can beer
1 tablespoon butter, melted

Preheat oven to 400 degrees. In large bowl, combine all ingredients. Mix well. Pour mixture into greased muffin pan. Bake 15 to 20 minutes. Makes 6 biscuits.

WONDERFUL BUTTER BISCUITS

1 cup self-rising flour

½ cup butter, softened

½ cup sour cream

Preheat oven to 400 degrees. In medium bowl, combine flour and butter. Mix well. Add sour cream. Blend well. Place spoonfuls of batter in greased muffin cups until half full. Bake 10 to 12 minutes or until golden brown.

LAYER HAM BISCUITS

1 (5 count) can tender layers biscuits

5 small slices of ham

1 tablespoon butter or margarine

Preheat oven to 400 degrees. Place biscuits on baking sheet. Pull half of layer off biscuits. Put 1 slice of ham on each biscuit. Put layers back on biscuits. Brush butter on top of each biscuit. Bake 8 to 10 minutes. Makes 5 biscuits.

MORNING TREAT BISCUITS

¼ cup chopped pecans

¼ cup packed brown sugar

1 (5 count) can biscuits

¼ cup melted butter

Preheat oven to 350 degrees. In small bowl, combine pecans and sugar. Dip each biscuit in butter then in sugar mixture. Place on baking sheet. Bake 8 to 10 minutes.

GREEN CHILE BISCUITS

  1 cup Bisquick®
  ½ cup shredded cheddar cheese
  2 tablespoons diced green chiles
  ¼ cup cold water
  4 teaspoons butter, melted
  ½ teaspoon garlic powder

Preheat oven to 450 degrees. In small bowl, combine Bisquick, cheese, and chiles. Add water, mix well. Drop mixture by tablespoon onto greased baking sheet, forming 6 biscuits. In small bowl, combine butter and garlic. Brush on biscuits. Bake 8 to 10 minutes or until golden brown.

BUTTER BASTED BISCUITS

  ½ cup self-rising flour
  ½ tablespoon sugar
  ½ cup milk
  2 tablespoons butter, melted

Preheat oven to 450 degrees. In small bowl, combine flour and sugar, mix well. Add milk, mix. On floured surface, pat dough to ½-inch thickness, cut into 4 squares. Coat each biscuit with butter. Place on baking sheet. Bake 10 minutes or until golden brown.

TO REFRESHEN BISCUITS PLACE THEM IN A WELL-DAMPENED PAPER BAG, TWIST IT CLOSED, AND PLACE IN THE OVEN AT 300 DEGREES UNTIL BAG IS HOT.

RAISIN TOPPED BISCUITS

¼ cup raisins

¼ cup packed brown sugar

1 (5 count) can refrigerated biscuits

¼ cup melted butter

Preheat oven to 350 degrees. In small bowl, combine raisins and brown sugar. Mix well. Dip each biscuit in butter then dip in mixture. Place on baking sheet. Bake 8 to 10 minutes. Makes 5 biscuits.

BLUEBERRY MUFFINS

1 cup plus 2 tablespoons from 7 ounce box Jiffy® blueberry muffin mix

2 tablespoons milk

1 egg white

Preheat oven to 400 degrees. In small bowl, combine all ingredients. Mix until blended. Spoon batter into 3 or 4 greased muffin cups. Bake 13 to 15 minutes or until golden brown.

CHEESY SAUSAGE MUFFINS

1 cup self-rising flour

¼ cup finely grated cheddar cheese

½ cup cooked, crumbled, breakfast sausage

½ cup milk

2 tablespoons vegetable oil

1 egg

Preheat oven to 400 degrees. In small bowl, combine flour, cheese, and sausage, mix well. Make a well in center of mixture. In small bowl, combine milk, oil, and egg. Add to flour mixture. Mix until combined but lumpy. Pour into 6 greased muffin cups. Bake 15 to 20 minutes or until golden brown.

NICE TOUCH DINNER ROLLS

    1 teaspoon butter, softened
    1 teaspoon mayonnaise
    1 teaspoon grated parmesan cheese
    4 brown and serve rolls

Preheat oven to 350 degrees. In small bowl, combine all ingredients, except rolls. Mix well. Place rolls on baking sheet. Spread mixture over top. Bake 8 to 10 minutes.

MAYONNAISE ROLLS

    1 cup self-rising flour
    ⅓ cup milk
    3 tablespoons mayonnaise

Preheat oven to 400 degrees. In medium bowl, combine all ingredients. Mix lightly. Drop mixture by tablespoon onto baking sheet coated with cooking spray. Bake 10 to 12 minutes or until golden brown.

IT'S QUICK & EASY ROLLS

    1 cup self-rising flour
    ½ cup milk
    1 teaspoon sugar
    2 tablespoons mayonnaise

Preheat oven to 350 degrees. In medium bowl, combine flour and milk. Add sugar and mayonnaise. Blend well. Pour into greased muffin pan. Bake for 12 to 15 minutes.

CARAMEL PECAN ROLLS

1 tablespoon caramel topping
¼ cup broken pecans
¼ teaspoon cinnamon
1 tablespoon sugar
1 (5 count) tube refrigerated biscuits
2 tablespoons milk

Preheat oven to 375 degrees. Spoon caramel topping into 4 muffin cups, sprinkle with nuts. In small bowl, combine cinnamon and sugar. Cut biscuits into 4 pieces. Dip biscuit pieces in milk, toss in sugar mixture, place in muffin cups. Bake 12 minutes or until golden brown.

COLD OVEN POPOVERS

2 eggs
1 cup milk
1 tablespoon butter, melted
1 cup self rising flour
¼ teaspoon salt

Butter 1 muffin pan, set aside. In large bowl, combine all ingredients. Mix well. Half fill muffin pan cups. Put in cold oven and set heat to 450 degrees. Bake 15 minutes. Reduce heat to 350 degrees. Bake 15 to 20 minutes or until golden and crisp on the outside. Note: This recipe is great for guests. Makes 10.

MEXICAN CORNBREAD

  1 cup self-rising cornmeal

  ½ cup milk

  1 egg

  2 tablespoons canned chopped green chiles

  ¼ cup shredded Mexican cheese

  ⅛ teaspoon red pepper

Preheat oven to 400 degrees. In medium bowl, combine all ingredients. Mix lightly. Pour mixture into 1-quart baking dish, coated with cooking spray. Bake 20 minutes.

FRIED CORNBREAD

  1 cup self-rising cornmeal

  ⅓ cup milk

  1 egg

  1 tablespoon melted butter

  Oil

In medium bowl, combine all ingredients, except oil. Mix lightly. Drop mixture by tablespoon in skillet with little oil. Brown on both sides.

**TO KEEP BUGS OUT OF YOUR FLOUR, PLACE AN
UNWRAPPED STICK OF SPEARMINT GUM IN THE
FLOUR BAG.**

GOLDEN CHEESE CORNBREAD

- 1 cup self-rising cornmeal
- ½ cup milk
- 1 egg
- 1 teaspoon sugar
- 2 tablespoons butter, melted
- ¼ cup shredded cheddar cheese

Preheat oven to 400 degrees. In medium bowl, combine all ingredients. Mix lightly. Pour mixture into 1-quart baking dish, coated with cooking spray. Bake 20 minutes.

SPOON DROP HUSH PUPPIES

- 1 cup self-rising cornmeal
- ⅓ cup milk
- 1 egg
- 1 teaspoon sugar
- 2 tablespoons diced onion

In medium bowl, combine all ingredients. Mix well. Mixture will be stiff. Drop by heaping teaspoonful into deep fat fryer with hot oil. Cook until golden brown.

ITALIAN BREADSTICKS

2 tablespoons grated parmesan cheese

1½ teaspoons sesame seeds

2 teaspoons dried Italian seasoning

4 frozen bread dough dinner rolls, thawed

¼ cup butter, melted

Preheat oven to 425 degrees. In small bowl, combine cheese, sesame seeds, and Italian seasoning. Mix well. Roll each roll into rope 8 inches long. Place on baking sheet with nonstick cooking spray. Brush tops and sides with butter. Sprinkle mixture over rolls. Bake 10 minutes or until golden brown. Makes 4 breadsticks.

ONE SLICE GRILLED CHEESE

2 slices bread, lightly toasted

2 teaspoons butter or margarine

2 slices American cheese

Place toast on baking sheet. Spread butter over top. Place 1 slice cheese on each slice. Broil until cheese melts. Note: Great with soup.

DAY OLD FRENCH TOAST

2 eggs, slightly beaten

¼ teaspoon salt

1 teaspoon sugar

2 tablespoons milk

2 or 4 slices day old bread

In shallow dish, combine all ingredients, except bread. Soak each slice of bread until soft. In medium skillet, fry bread in a little oil, over medium high heat until golden brown on both sides. Serve with syrup or jelly.

Note: French toast is always better if bread is a little old.

BEST WAY CINNAMON TOAST

2 slices white bread
2 tablespoons butter, softened
1 tablespoon cinnamon
3 tablespoons sugar

Toast bread. Butter one side. In small bowl, combine cinnamon and sugar. Mix well. Spoon mixture over butter side of toast. Place on baking sheet. Place under broiler. Broil until sugar melts.

CINNAMON BUTTER

½ cup butter, softened
1 tablespoon packed brown sugar
1 teaspoon sugar
½ teaspoon ground cinnamon

In small bowl, combine all ingredients. Mix well. Use on toast or muffins.

GARLIC BUTTER SPREAD

⅓ cup butter or margarine
¼ teaspoon garlic powder

In small bowl, combine all ingredients. Mix well. Let stand 30 minutes before serving.

PIPING HOT BUTTER

½ cup butter, softened
1 tablespoon salsa
1 teaspoon chopped cilantro
⅛ teaspoon red pepper

In small bowl, combine all ingredients. Mix well. Use on cornbread, breadsticks, etc.

FRENCH ONION SPREAD

⅓ cup butter or margarine, softened
2 tablespoons diced onion
⅛ teaspoon red pepper

In small bowl, combine all ingredients. Mix well. Cover. Refrigerate until ready to use. Makes ⅓ cup.

PINEAPPLE CREAM SPREAD

1 (8 ounce) package cream cheese
3 tablespoons crushed pineapple
1 teaspoon milk

In small bowl, combine all ingredients. Mix well. Serve with crackers.

**DIP A SPOON IN HOT WATER WHEN
MEASURING SHORTENING OR BUTTER
AND THE FAT WILL SLIP OUT MORE EASILY.**

SYRUP IS BETTER HOMEMADE

1 cup packed brown sugar
½ cup water
1 tablespoon butter
¼ teaspoon maple flavoring

In medium saucepan, combine all ingredients. Over medium heat bring to a boil. Boil 2 to 3 minutes. Makes 1 cup.

BREAD TOPPING FOR CASSEROLES

4 tablespoons butter
1 cup fresh bread crumbs

In medium skillet, melt butter over medium heat. Add bread crumbs. Cook and stir until crumbs are lightly toasted and butter is absorbed.

Note: Excellent topping for casseroles.

SELF-RISING CORNMEAL

1 cup regular cornmeal
1½ teaspoons baking powder
½ teaspoon salt

In small bowl, combine all ingredients. Mix well. Makes 1 cup.

SELF-RISING FLOUR

    1 cup flour
    1½ teaspoons baking powder
    ½ teaspoon salt

In small bowl, combine all ingredients. Mix well. Makes 1 cup.

PIZZA SAUCE FOR BREADSTICKS

    ¾ cup pizza sauce
    ½ cup shredded mozzarella cheese
    2 tablespoons diced pepperoni

In small bowl, combine all ingredients. Mix well. Cover. Microwave until hot. Serve with breadsticks.

NOTES

Desserts

PRIZE WINNING PINEAPPLE DOUGHNUT

State Fair

> 1 plain cake doughnut
> 2 teaspoons butter, softened
> 3 tablespoons packed brown sugar
> 2 slices pineapple, drained
> 2 maraschino cherries

Cut doughnut in half. Place on microwave safe plate. Spread butter over doughnuts. On each doughnut slice sprinkle 1½ tablespoons brown sugar over butter. Place pineapple slice on top. Place cherry in center. Microwave 15 to 20 seconds or until heated through.

MOCK APPLE COBBLER

> 12 vanilla wafer cookies
> ½ cup chunky cinnamon applesauce
> 2 tablespoons whipped topping

In 2 bowls, layer cookies. Top with applesauce. Microwave 15 to 20 seconds. Top with whipped topping.

IF CHOCOLATE MORSELS LOOK GRAY ON THE SURFACE, THEIR QUALITY IS NOT AFFECTED AND DISAPPEARS WHEN THE CHOCOLATE IS MELTED.

STRAWBERRY SHORTCAKE

    6 strawberries, sliced
    2 tablespoons sugar, divided
    ½ cup baking mix
    2 tablespoons buttermilk
    ½ tablespoon butter, melted
    ½ cup whipped topping

Preheat oven to 400 degrees. In small bowl, combine strawberries and 1 tablespoon sugar. Mix well. Set aside. In medium bowl, combine baking mix, buttermilk, 1 tablespoon sugar, and butter until moist. On ungreased baking sheet form two biscuits. Bake 12 minutes or until golden brown. Cool. Split biscuits, layer strawberries and whipped topping. Garnish with additional whipped topping and sliced strawberries if desired.

CHOCOLATE CAKE

    ¾ cup from 9 ounce box Jiffy® chocolate
        cake mix
    1 egg white
    ¼ cup water

Preheat oven to 350 degrees. In small bowl, combine all ingredients. Mix well. Pour into 3 or 4 greased muffin cups. Bake 15 to 18 minutes.

NO EGG CHOCOLATE CAKE

        1 cup flour
        ½ cup sugar
        ¼ cup baking cocoa powder
        1 teaspoon baking soda
        ½ cup Miracle Whip®
        ½ cup boiling water
        ½ teaspoon vanilla

Preheat oven to 350 degrees. In medium bowl, combine flour, sugar, cocoa, and baking soda. Mix well. In small bowl, combine remaining ingredients. Mix well. Add liquid to dry ingredients. Mix until smooth. Grease and flour 4 to 6 muffin cups. Fill cup to ¾ full. Bake 20 minutes or until toothpick inserted comes out clean.

IT'S A SECRET CHOCOLATE CAKE

If I Gotta Cook Make It Quick! Cookbook

        1 box chocolate cake mix
        ½ cup unsweetened cocoa
        3 eggs
    1½ cups water
        1 cup Miracle Whip®

Preheat oven to 350 degrees. In large bowl, combine cake mix and cocoa. Mix well. Add eggs, water, and Miracle Whip. Beat at medium speed with electric mixer until blended. Pour mixture into greased and floured 13 x 9 x 2-inch baking pan. Bake 30 to 40 minutes. Makes 12 servings.

CREAM CHEESE FROSTING

1 (8 ounce) package cream cheese, softened
¼ cup butter
2 cups confectioner's sugar
1 teaspoon vanilla

In medium bowl, combine all ingredients. Beat until smooth. Note: very good on spice cakes, carrot cakes, and fruit.

LAST MINUTE GUEST PIE

5 or 6 macaroons
¼ cup chocolate syrup
1 quart vanilla ice cream, slightly softened
2 tablespoons chocolate syrup
¼ cup chopped almonds

In 8-inch pie plate, press macaroons to make crust. Drizzle chocolate syrup over crust. Spread ice cream evenly over top. Freeze 20 minutes. Drizzle syrup and sprinkle nuts over ice cream.

EASY TO MAKE PIE CRUST

1 cup flour
3 tablespoons sugar
½ cup margarine, softened

Preheat oven to 350 degrees. In medium bowl, combine all ingredients. Mix well. Press dough into 8-inch pie pan. Bake 8 to 10 minutes or until golden brown. Makes 1 pie crust.

MILE HIGH MERINGUE

4 egg whites, room temperature
½ teaspoon cream of tartar
8 tablespoons sugar

In large bowl, add egg whites and cream of tartar. Beat with electric mixer on medium speed until soft peaks form. Gradually add sugar 1 tablespoon at a time, beating on high speed until soft peaks form. Spread over pie. Bake as directed in pie recipe.

FUDGY BROWNIE CRUST

1¼ cups chocolate wafer crumbs
2 tablespoons sugar
2 tablespoons butter or margarine, melted
1 egg white

Preheat oven to 350 degrees. In blender, combine wafer crumbs, sugar, and butter, pulse until moistened. Press mixture into 9-inch pie pan. Bake 8 to 10 minutes or until lightly browned. Cool before filling. Makes 1 pie crust.

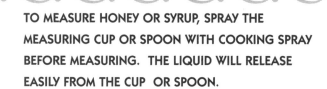

TO MEASURE HONEY OR SYRUP, SPRAY THE
MEASURING CUP OR SPOON WITH COOKING SPRAY
BEFORE MEASURING. THE LIQUID WILL RELEASE
EASILY FROM THE CUP OR SPOON.

APPLE PIE QUESADILLAS

> 2 (6-inch) flour tortillas
> 1½ teaspoons butter or margarine
> ⅓ cup diced apples from canned pie filling
> ¼ cup finely shredded cheddar cheese
> 1 teaspoon sugar
> ¼ teaspoon cinnamon

Butter outside of each tortilla. In medium skillet, place 1 tortilla, butter side down. Spread apple over tortilla to ½ inch from edge. Sprinkle cheese over apples. Top with remaining tortilla, butter side up. Sprinkle with sugar and cinnamon. Over medium high heat cook until golden brown.

Cooking Tip: Use your contact grill.

CINNAMON CRISPS

> ½ cup sugar
> ¾ teaspoon cinnamon
> 2 (6-inch) flour tortillas, cut in 2-inch strips
> Oil for frying

In small bowl, combine sugar and cinnamon. Mix well. In large skillet, heat 1 inch of oil, over high heat. When oil is hot, fry tortilla strips until golden brown on each side. Drain on paper towel. While still hot, sprinkle sugar mixture over both sides of tortilla.

LICKETY SPLIT TREATS

1 (6 ounce) package semi sweet chocolate
½ cup Spanish peanuts
1 cup chow mien noodles

In medium bowl, add chocolate. Microwave on high 2 minutes or until chocolate melts. Add nuts and noodles. Mix well. Drop mixture with tablespoon on wax paper. Place in refrigerator until chocolate is set.

CHOCOLATE DELIGHT SQUARES

1½ cups creamy peanut butter
1½ cups confectioner's sugar
1½ teaspoons vanilla
1 (18 ounce) roll refrigerated chocolate chip cookies

Preheat oven to 350 degrees. In medium bowl, combine peanut butter, sugar, and vanilla. Mix well. Cut cookie dough in half crosswise. With floured fingers press half of dough in bottom of ungreased 9-inch square pan. Press peanut butter mixture evenly over dough. Crumble remaining dough over mixture evenly as possible. Bake 30 minutes. Cool. Refrigerate until chilled. Cut into bars.

WHEN MAILING COOKIES, PACK THEM IN
UNBUTTERED AND UNSALTED POPCORN TO
HELP KEEP COOKIES FROM CRUMBLING.

CAN'T BE A COOKIE

Get Me out of the Kitchen

2 cups sugar

1 cup peanut butter

1 teaspoon vanilla

1 egg

Preheat oven to 350 degrees. In medium bowl, combine all ingredients. Mix well. Drop mixture by heaping teaspoon onto greased cookie sheet. Using a fork, criss cross each cookie. Bake 10 minutes. Cool on wire rack. Note this recipe calls for no flour.

BUTTER COOKIES

¾ cup butter (do not use margarine), softened

⅓ cup confectioner's sugar

4½ teaspoons sugar

2 teaspoons almond extract

1⅓ cups flour

¼ teaspoon salt

Preheat oven to 325 degrees. In medium bowl, cream butter and sugars. Add extract. Mix well. In small bowl, combine flour and salt. Gradually add to butter mixture, beating constantly. Mix well. Refrigerate 1 hour. Roll dough between wax paper to ⅛-inch thickness. Cut into shapes. Using floured spatula, transfer to ungreased baking sheet, 1 inch apart. Bake 12 to 15 minutes or until edges begin to brown. Makes 9 cookies.

CHEWY MACAROONS

7 ounces sweetened condensed milk

1 teaspoon vanilla

1 (7 ounce) package flaked coconut

Preheat oven to 325 degrees. In medium bowl, combine all ingredients. Mix well. Drop mixture by tablespoon on greased and floured baking sheet. Slightly flatten each mound. Bake 15 minutes or until golden. Makes 12 cookies.

PEANUT BUTTER BALLS

¼ cup creamy peanut butter

6 tablespoons dry powded milk

2 tablespoons confectioner's sugar

2 tablespoons honey

In small bowl, combine all ingredients. Mix until smooth. Form 1½-inch size balls. Refrigerate at least 30 minutes before serving.

CHOCOLATE MOUSSE

¾ cup heavy whipping cream

1½ tablespoons sugar

¾ teaspoon vanilla

2 tablespoons plus 2 teaspoons chocolate syrup

1½ tablespoons cocoa

In medium chilled bowl, beat cream until soft peaks form. Add sugar and vanilla, beat until stiff peaks form. Fold in syrup and cocoa. Refrigerate until serving.

RICE PUDDING

½ cup uncooked long grain rice

½ cup water

1 cup plus 2 tablespoons milk

6 tablespoons sugar

2 tablespoons raisins

1 teaspoon cinnamon

In small sauce pan, add rice and water. Over medium high heat bring to a boil. Reduce heat to low. Cover. Simmer 8 to 10 minutes or until liquid is absorbed. Add milk, sugar, raisins, and cinnamon. Over low heat cook uncovered, stirring occasionally, 30 minutes or until rice is tender.

BIG HIT BERRY CRUMBLE

½ (21 ounce) can cherry pie filling

1 cup fresh or frozen raspberries

7 ounces sweetened condensed milk

¾ cup granola

In medium saucepan, combine cherry pie filling, milk, and raspberries. Over low heat cook until hot. Simmer 1 minute. Spoon mixture into 1-quart baking dish. Sprinkle granola over top. Serve warm.

WHEN MAKING A PIE THAT CALLS FOR
MERINGUE, BE SURE THE MERINGUE TOUCHES
THE EDGES OF THE CRUST. IT WILL HELP KEEP
THE MERINGUE FROM SHRINKING.

BERRIES AND CREAM TRIFLES

1 cup cubed angel food cake
½ cup fresh blueberries
½ cup sliced strawberries
1⅓ cups whipped topping

In medium bowl, combine all ingredients. Mix well. Chill.

BLUEBERRY CRUNCH

2 cups frozen blueberries
½ cup packed brown sugar
6 tablespoons flour
6 tablespoons uncooked oats
¼ cup melted butter

Preheat oven to 350 degrees. In 1½-quart baking dish, add blueberries. In small bowl, combine remaining ingredients. Blend well. Sprinkle mixture over blueberries. Bake 20 to 30 minutes.

FRUIT & FLUFF

2 ounces cream cheese, softened
½ cup sour cream
1 tablespoon sugar
1½ teaspoons milk
Assorted berries

In small bowl, combine cream cheese, sour cream, sugar, and milk. Mix well. Place berries in two bowls, spoon cream mixture over top.

MIXED FRUIT & YOGURT

> 4 strawberries, sliced
> 1 medium apple, diced
> 1 tangerine, peeled, chopped
> ½ cup halved green grapes
> 1 cup vanilla yogurt

In medium bowl, combine all ingredients. Mix well.

YOGURT PARFAITS

> ⅓ cup granola
> 1 (6 ounce) vanilla yogurt
> 1 cup raspberries

In two parfait glasses, layer granola, yogurt, fruit, yogurt, and granola.

LEMON BERRY PARFAITS

> 1 (8 ounce) carton lemon yogurt
> ¾ cup frozen raspberries, thawed
> Whipped topping

In two parfait glasses, alternate layer of yogurt and raspberries. Garnish with whipped topping.

**TO PREVENT ICE CREAM CONES
FROM DRIPPING, STUFF A
MARSHMALLOW IN THE BOTTOM.**

BERRIES & CREAM DESSERT

1½ cups blueberries

¼ cup sour cream

2 tablespoons brown sugar

Preheat oven to broil. Place berries in 2 oven proof single serving dishes. Spread sour cream over berries. Sprinkle with brown sugar. Broil 6 inches from heat, 4 minutes or until sugar is melted.

WHITE CHOCOLATE COVERED BERRIES

4 ounces white chocolate, chopped

1 cup heavy cream

¼ teaspoon almond extract

2 cups frozen berries, slightly thawed

In double boiler, heat chocolate and cream, over low heat, stirring occasionally. When melted, remove from heat, add extract, mix well. Place berries in 2 dishes. Pour chocolate over top.

EASY APPLESAUCE

2 Macintosh apples, peeled, cored, sliced

¼ cup water

½ teaspoon sugar

¼ teaspoon cinnamon

In small saucepan, add apples and water. Over medium high heat bring to boil. Reduce heat to low. Cover. Cook 10 minutes. Uncover, increase heat to medium. Cook 20 minutes or until apples are soft. Remove from heat. Mash with fork. Add sugar and cinnamon, mix well.

BAKED APPLES

> 2 medium Granny Smith apples, cored
> ½ teaspoon cinnamon
> 12 miniature marshmallows
> 2 tablespoons packed brown sugar

Preheat oven to 350 degrees. Place apples on individual pieces of aluminum foil. Sprinkle cinnamon down core of each apple. Alternate layering brown sugar then marshmallows. Wrap foil around apples. Place in 9 x 9-inch baking dish. Bake 30 to 35 minutes.

CARAMEL APPLES

> 2 apples, cored, sliced
> ½ cup caramel ice cream topping
> 1 tablespoon chopped peanuts

Place apples on two plates. Drizzle caramel over top. Sprinkle with nuts.

NUTS ABOUT BANANAS

> 2 medium bananas, sliced
> 2 tablespoons salted peanuts
> 1 tablespoon flaked coconut
> 1 tablespoon honey

In medium bowl, combine all ingredients. Mix well.

THE FIRST POPSICLE WAS
ACCIDENTALLY MADE BY 11 YEAR OLD
FRANK EPPERSON IN 1905.

FROSTY DIPPED BANANAS

¼ pound milk chocolate

2 wooden sticks

1 large banana, halved lengthwise

½ cup chopped peanuts

In small saucepan, melt chocolate over very low heat. Stir constantly. Pour into shallow dish. Insert wooden sticks into banana halves. Roll in chocolate, then in nuts. Place on baking sheet covered with wax paper. Freeze.

BANANAS FOSTER FOR TWO

3 tablespoons butter

¼ cup packed brown sugar

1 banana, sliced

½ teaspoon rum flavoring

2 scoops vanilla ice cream

In small skillet, melt butter over low heat. Add brown sugar, cook until sugar is melted, stirring constantly. Boil 1 minute. Add bananas and rum flavoring. Cook 2 minutes. Mix well. Place ice cream on 2 plates. Spoon sauce over ice cream.

SWEET & TART GRAPEFRUIT

1 ruby grapefruit, halved

2 tablespoons packed brown sugar

2 tablespoons sweetened coconut flakes

Preheat oven to broil. Place grapefruit on baking sheet. Sprinkle brown sugar then coconut over top of grapefruit. Broil 3 minutes or until coconut is toasted.

DE-LIGHT-FUL DESSERT

4 ice cream sandwiches
¾ cup whipped topping
1 large Butterfinger® candy bar, crushed

In 1½-quart glass dish, line bottom with ice cream. Spread whipped topping over ice cream sandwiches. Sprinkle Butterfinger crumbs over top. Cover. Freeze until ready to serve.

APPLE SAUCE ICE CREAM

2 cups diced peeled Granny Smith apples
¼ cup packed brown sugar
¼ cup chopped walnuts
1 tablespoon butter
1 teaspoon cinnamon
2 scoops vanilla ice cream

In small saucepan, combine all ingredients, except ice cream. Over medium high heat bring to a boil. Reduce heat to low. Simmer 20 minutes. Cool. Place ice cream in 2 bowls, spoon sauce over top.

LEMON ICE

1 cup heavy whipping cream
½ cup sugar
2 tablespoons plus 2 teaspoons lemon juice
½ tablespoon grated lemon peel

In medium bowl, combine all ingredients, mix until sugar dissolves. Pour into 2 freezer proof dishes, freeze at least 4 hours. Remove 15 minutes before serving.

PEACH SORBET

2 cups chopped frozen peaches

1 tablespoon sugar

½ teaspoon lemon juice

In blender, combine all ingredients. Cover. Blend until smooth. Serve immediately or freeze.

STRAWBERRIES & CREAM SHERBET

1 cup sliced fresh strawberries

½ cup sugar

½ cup half-and-half

In blender, combine all ingredients. Cover. Blend until smooth. Pour into individual serving dishes. Freeze. Remove 15 minutes before serving.

PEANUT BUTTER SUNDAES

6 tablespoons packed brown sugar

2 tablespoons milk

1 tablespoon plus 1 teaspoon corn syrup

1 teaspoon butter or margarine

1 tablespoon plus 1 teaspoon creamy peanut butter

2 scoops vanilla ice cream

In small saucepan, combine sugar, milk, syrup, and butter. Over medium heat cook until sugar is dissolved. Add peanut butter. Mix well. Cover. Chill. In 2 bowls place ice cream. Drizzle peanut butter mixture over top.

PEANUT CLUSTERS

½ cup milk chocolate chips

¼ cup creamy peanut butter

¾ cup roasted peanuts

In small bowl, melt chips in microwave, 30 seconds to 1 minute or until melted. Add peanut butter. Mix well. Add peanuts. Mix to coat. Drop by teaspoon onto wax paper. Refrigerate to set.

COOKIES & CRÈME FUDGE

9 ounces white chocolate baking squares

7 ounces sweetened condensed milk

10 chocolate crème filled sandwich cookies

In medium saucepan, combine white chocolate squares and milk. Over low heat melt mixture. Add cookies. Mix well. Spread in buttered 8-inch pie plate. Chill until firm.

TRIM THE FAT FUDGE

1½ cups reduced fat semi sweet chocolate chips

7 ounces fat free sweetened condensed milk

1 tablespoon cocoa powder

½ teaspoon instant coffee crystals

½ teaspoon vanilla

In medium saucepan, combine chocolate chips, milk, and cocoa. Over low heat cook until chips melt. Add coffee crystals and vanilla. Mix well. Spread mixture in buttered 8-inch pie plate. Chill until firm.

QUICK FIXING FUDGE

    1½ cups semi sweet chocolate chips

     7 ounces sweetened condensed milk

    ¼ cup chopped walnuts

    ¾ teaspoon vanilla

In medium saucepan, combine chocolate chips and milk. Over low heat cook until chips melt. Add nuts and vanilla. Mix well. Spread mixture in buttered 8-inch pie pan. Chill until firm.

HOLIDAY FUDGE

    ½ cup plus 2 tablespoons fresh or frozen cranberries

    ¼ cup light corn syrup

     1 cup semi-sweet chocolate chips

    ¼ cup confectioner's sugar

    ¼ cup chopped walnuts

     2 tablespoons evaporated milk

    ½ teaspoon vanilla

In medium saucepan, add cranberries and syrup. Over medium high heat bring to a boil. Boil 5 to 6 minutes, stirring often. Remove from heat. Add remaining ingredients, mix until chips are melted. Pour into buttered aluminum foil lined 8-inch baking dish.

MARSHMALLOW FUDGE

¾ cup sugar

⅓ cup evaporated milk

1 tablespoon butter or margarine

1 cup miniature marshmallows

½ cup plus 3 tablespoons milk chocolate chips

½ teaspoon vanilla

In small saucepan, add sugar, milk and butter. Over medium high heat bring to a rolling boil, stirring constantly. Boil 3 to 4 minutes. Remove from heat. Stir in marshmallows, chips, and vanilla. Mix until chips are melted. Pour into buttered aluminum foil lined 4-inch dish. Refrigerate 1 hour or until firm.

MILK CHOCOLATE DROPS

1 cup milk chocolate chips

½ teaspoon shortening

¼ cup raisins

¼ cup walnuts

In small saucepan, combine chocolate chips and shortening. Over low heat cook until chocolate chips melt. Add raisins and walnuts. Mix well. Drop mixture by teaspoonful onto wax paper. Chill until firm.

MAKE CANDY ON DRY DAYS. CANDY DOES NOT SET AS WELL ON HUMID OR RAINY DAYS.

CHOCOLATE & PEANUT TOFFEE

½ cup dry roasted peanuts, divided
½ cup butter
½ cup sugar
¼ cup packed brown sugar
1 tablespoon light corn syrup
½ cup plus 3 tablespoons milk chocolate chips

Line 9 x 9-inch baking pan with aluminum foil. In small saucepan, melt butter over medium heat. Stir in sugar, brown sugar, and syrup. Bring to a boil. Cook 6 minutes, stirring occasionally. Pour mixture evenly over ¼ cup peanuts. Sprinkle remaining nuts over top. Sprinkle chips on top. Refrigerate 1 hour or until set.

Techniques, Tips & Table Manners

ADAPT MOST RECIPES TO A SLOW COOKER FOR HASSLE FREE COOKING

Crock Pot® And Slow Cookers Are The Same

YOU CAN PREPARE just about any type of meal in a Slow Cooker. There is nothing easier then putting ingredients into a Slow Cooker in the morning, and coming home to a hot cooked meal. Here are some tips to help adapt your recipes for successful cooking in your Slow Cooker. Several factors can affect your recipes, so REMEMBER THESE TIPS.

Cooking time in all recipes are approximations, affected by how much food is in the cooker, humidity, the temperature of the ingredients when you add them; so note that cooking times in the recipes are ranges only.

To make cleanup easier, spray the inside of the Slow Cooker with non-stick cooking spray before adding food.

Meats will not brown in a Slow Cooker. If a recipes calls for meat to be browned, brown it in a skillet. The recipe will be better, it will enhance the flavor and decrease fat.

A Slow Cooker is great for tougher cuts of meat.

It is always better to thaw meat before placing it in the Slow Cooker. It will cook faster.

Fill cooker between half and two-thirds full.

Add vegetables to cooker first, then add meat. Vegetables cook slower than meat.

Cut vegetables in smaller pieces to ensure proper cooking.

Do not add as much water as regular recipes indicate. Use about half the recommended amount, unless it calls for rice or pasta. Liquids don't boil away as in conventional cooking.

If recipe calls for raw rice, add ¼ cup extra liquid per ¼ cup of raw rice

If recipe calls for pasta or rice, cook until slightly tender.

If recipe calls for dry beans, it is best to cook beans before adding to recipe.

In the last hour of cooking it is better to add milk, sour cream or cream to the recipe. Dairy products tend to curdle over long cooking periods. Condensed cream of soup or evaporated milk can be substituted in some recipes.

Processed cheeses tend to work better in Slow Cookers than natural cheese.

Juices can be thickened by adding corn starch during the last hour of cooking. Turn heat to high.

It is best to add ground seasoning near the end of cooking.

Cooking Guide for Adapting Recipes

Time Guide

IF RECIPE SAYS COOK	COOK ON LOW	COOK ON HIGH
15 to 30 minutes	4 to 6 hours	1½ to 2 hours
35 to 45 minutes	6 to 10 hours	3 to 4 hours
50 minutes to 3 hours	8 to 15 hours	4 to 6 hours

Slow Cooker Don'ts

• DON'T remove the lid during cooking unless recipe calls for it. Every time you lift the lid you will slow the cooking time by 20 to 30 minutes.

• DON'T leave food in the Crock Pot®. Remove food within one hour.

• DON'T reheat food in a Crock Pot® because it takes too much time for food to reach a safe temperature.

• DON'T add water to clean the cooker until it has cooled.

• DON'T use metal utensils; use rubber, plastic or wood to avoid damaging interior of the Crock Pot®s.

HERBS AND SPICES ARE USED FOR WHAT?

BASIL — Good with stews, roast beef, ground beef, lamb, fish, vegetables, and omelets.

BAY LEAVES — Has a pungent flavor. Good in seafood, stews, and vegetable dishes.

CARAWAY — Use in breads, soups, cakes, cheese, and sauerkraut.

CHIVES — Good in salads, fish, soups, and potatoes.

CILANTRO — Southwestern dishes, rice, beans, salads, fish, and chicken.

CURRY POWDER — A combination of spices that give a distinct flavor to meat, poultry, fish, and vegetables.

DILL — Both seeds and leaves may be used. Leaves can be used as a garnish or cooked with soup, fish, potatoes, and beans.

FENNEL — Has a hot, sweet flavor. Small quantities are used in pies and baked goods, and the leaves can be boiled with fish.

GINGER — It is a pungent root and is used in pickles, cakes, cookies, preserves, soups, and meat dishes.

MARJORAM — It adds flavor to stew, stuffing, lamb, fish, poultry, and omelets.

MINT — It is great in beverages, soup, peas, carrots, lamb, cheese, preserves and fruit desserts.

OREGANO — It can be used whole or ground, in pizza, tomato juice, fish, eggs, omelets, stew, gravy, poultry, and vegetables.

PAPRIKA — A bright red pepper that is used as a garnish for potatoes, salads, and eggs, and as a spice used in meat, vegetables, and soup.

PARSLEY — Can be used dried as seasoning or garnish. Use in fish, soup, meat, stuffing, and mixed greens.

ROSEMARY — It can be used to season fish, stuffing, beef, lamb, poultry, onions, eggs, bread, and potatoes. It is great in dressings.

SAFFRON — It is used in breads, soup, rice, and chicken.

SAGE — May be used in stuffing, fish, omelets, poultry, tomato juice, breads, and cheese spreads.

TARRAGON — Used in salads, sauces, fish, poultry, tomatoes, eggs, carrots, green beans, and dressing.

THYME — Leaves may be sprinkled on fish or poultry before baking or broiling.

COOKING TECHNIQUES

SEAR — To brown quickly over high heat

SAUTÉ — To fry lightly and quickly in a little hot oil while being frequently turned over.

ROAST — A dry-heat method of cooking meat or poultry in an oven.

BAKE — A dry heat for baking bread, pies or cake.

STEAM — To cook food over boiling water in a covered pan.

FRY — Pan frying is done in a small amount of oil. Deep frying is immersed in hot oil.

BOIL — To cook in liquid that is bubbling.

POACH — To gently cook in not quite simmering water or seasoned liquid.

GRILL — To cook on a grill or directly over an open flame.

SUBSTITUTIONS

Out Of This Ingredient? Then Substitute:

INGREDIENT	AMOUNT	SUBSTITUTE
Allspice	1 teaspoon	½ teaspoon cinnamon and ½ teaspoon ground cloves
Baking Powder	1 teaspoon	¼ teaspoon baking soda and 1 teaspoon cream of tartar
Broth-beef or chicken	1 cup	1 bouillon cube dissolved in 1 cup boiling water
Catsup	1 cup	1 cup tomato sauce, ½ cup sugar and 2 teaspoons vinegar
Chives, finely chopped	2 teaspoons	2 teaspoons finely chopped green onion tips
Chocolate chips-	1 ounce	1 ounce sweet cooking semi sweet chocolate
Cornstarch-for thickening	1 tablespoon	2 tablespoons all-purpose flour 4 to 6 teaspoons quick cooking tapioca
Cracker Crumbs	¾ cup	1 cup bread crumbs
Cream Cheese	1 cup	1 cup cottage cheese beaten until smooth
Dry Mustard	1 teaspoon	1 tablespoon prepared mustard
Flour, cake	1 cup sifted	1 cup minus 2 teaspoons all-purpose flour
Flour, self rising	1 cup	1 cup minus 2 teaspoons all-purpose flour plus 1½ teaspoons baking powder and ½ teaspoon salt

INGREDIENT	AMOUNT	SUBSTITUTE
Herbs, fresh	1 tablespoon	1 teaspoon dried herbs
Milk, sour	1 cup	1 tablespoon lemon juice and 1 cup milk
Milk, buttermilk	1 cup	1 cup plain yogurt
Milk, whole	1 cup	½ cup evaporated milk and ⅓ water
Onion, fresh	1 small	1 tablespoon minced onion, dehydrated
Sugar, brown	½ cup	2 tablespoons molasses in ½ cup granulated sugar
Sugar, confectioner's	1 cup	1 cup granulated sugar plus 1 teaspoon cornstarch
Sugar, maple	½ cup	1 cup maple syrup
Tomatoes, fresh	2 cups	1 (16 ounce) can diced tomatoes
Tomato sauce	1 (15-ounce) can	1 (6-ounce) can tomato paste plus cup water
Wine	1 cup	13 tablespoons water, 3 tablespoons lemon juice and 1 tablespoon sugar
Worcestershire sauce	1 teaspoon	1 teaspoon bottled steak sauce
Yogurt	1 cup	1 cup sour cream

IT MAKES HOW MUCH?

FOOD FOR INGREDIENTS	QUANTITY	YIELDS
Apple	1 medium	1 cup
Bread Crumbs	1 slice	¼ cup
Butter	1 stick	½ cup
Egg whites	8 to 10	1 cup
Egg yolks	10 to 12	1 cup
Noodles, uncooked	1½ cups	2 to 3 cups cooked
Macaroni, uncooked	1¼ cups	2½ cups cooked
Spaghetti	8 ounces	4½ cups cooked
Nuts, chopped	¼ pound	1 cup
Nuts, walnuts, unshelled	1 pound	1½ cups
Onion, chopped	1 medium	½ cup
Rice, regular	1 cup	3 cups cooked
Rice, wild	1 cup	4 cups cooked
Sugar, brown	1 pound	2½ cups
Sugar, white	1 pound	2 cups

MEASUREMENTS FOR COOKING

3 teaspoons .... 1 tablespoon

2 tablespoons .... 1 fluid ounce

4 tablespoons .... ¼ cup

5 tablespoons plus 1 teaspoon .... ⅓ cup

8 tablespoons .... ½ cup

16 tablespoons .... 1 cup

Dash .... less than ⅛ teaspoon

Pinch .... as much as can be taken between tip of fingers and thumb

HINTS TO MAKE COOKING EASY

1. If an egg cracks while being cooked in the shell, add a small amount of vinegar to the water to prevent the egg white from seeping from the shell.

2. Add 1 teaspoon of salt to cold water before boiling eggs to make them easier to peel.

3. Fresh lemon juice will remove onion scent form your hands.

4. Soak potatoes to be baked for 20 to 30 minutes to make them bake faster.

5. Freeze extra chopped onions, peppers and other vegetables for later use.

6. Marinate meat in sturdy plastic bag — no cleanup, no mess.

7. Use an egg slicer to quickly slice mushrooms

8. Keep knives sharp to reduce chopping time.

9. Spray the blade of the knife with cooking spray before cutting cheese or dried fruit. It will make cutting easier.

10. When measuring shortening, butter, etc., dip the spoon in hot water. The fat will slip out easily.

11. Cookie dough that is to be rolled is much easier to handle if it has been refrigerated for 15 to 30 minutes.

12. For scorched pans fill them halfway with water and ¼ cup baking soda. Boil until the burned portions loosen and float to the top.

13. Remove food burnt in a skillet by adding a drop of liquid dish soap, add water to fill halfway, bring to a boil.

14. Keep disinfecting wipes handy and clean as you cook.

TOP TIPS IN GRILLING

• Let beef stand a few minutes after grilling. You will have a tastier piece of meat.

• When handling steaks, use tongs or a spatula instead of a fork, so you won't pierce the meat during cooking and allow the juices to seep out.

• Zippered plastic food storage bags are great for mess free marinating.

• The sooner the grill is cleaned after using, the easier cleaning will be.

• To prevent food from sticking to the grill, spray the cold grill with cooking spray or brush with vegetable oil.

• Avoid over mixing ground beef before grilling.

• If using bamboo skewers, soak them in water for about an hour before grilling to prevent them from burning.

• Soaking corn in cold water helps tenderize it and helps prevent the husks from burning while grilling.

• If you don't have a grill basket, a sheet of heavy duty foil that has a few holes poked in it also works.

• Salt meats after grilling.

• Trim excess fat from meat before grilling.

- Tougher cuts of meat should be tenderized by marinating or pounding with a meat mallet.

- Do not return cooked meat to a plate that was in contact with raw meat.

- Barbecue sauce is best applied towards the end of cooking to prevent burning.

GRILLING IT RIGHT

Heating the Grill

Gas grills heat 5 to 10 minutes before cooking.

Charcoal grills, light coals approximately 30 to 45 minutes before putting meat on the grill.

Temperature of Coals

The temperature of the coals is important for successful grilling. If the coals are too hot, the outside of the food can become charred and overcooked before the inside is properly cooked.

Controlling Flare-ups

Flare-ups are caused by fat and meat juices dripping onto hot coals and causing sudden small blazes.

1. Raise grill rack.
2. Remove a few coals.
3. Spread the coals further apart.
4. Cover grill.
5. Remove food from grill.
6. Mist fire with water.

Equipment and Accessories to Have on Hand

1. A stiff wire brush or scraper for brushing and scraping away burnt on food from the bars or griddle.
2. Gas lighter for barbecues without an automatic lighter.

3. Long handled tongs for turning and moving food from the grill.

4. Meat turner for lifting hamburgers, fish, etc.

5. Long sharp knife for carving large pieces of meat.

6. Heatproof gloves.

7. Water spray bottle to subdue flare-ups.

Approximate Cooking Time

Most beef cuts are best grilled over medium heat.

Medium Rare to Medium

Ribeye steak
¾ inch — 6 to 8 minutes
1 inch — 11 to 14 minutes

**Porterhouse/
T-Bone Steak**
¾ inch — 10 to 12 minutes
1 inch — 14 to 16 minutes

Top Loin Steak
¾ inch — 10 to 12 minutes
1 inch — 15 to 18 minutes

Tenderloin Steak
1 inch — 13 to 15 minutes

Top Sirloin Steak
¾ inch to 1 inch — 13 to 16 minutes
Boneless 1 inch — 17 to 21 minutes

Flank Steak
1½ to 2 lb. — 17 to 20 minutes

Top Round Steak
¾ inch — 8 to 9 minutes

Ground Beef patties
¼ lb. — 11 to 13 minutes
½ lb. — 13 to 15 minutes

Grilling Time for Vegetables

5-10 minutes

Carrot pieces or small whole Carrots

Whole Mushrooms

New Potatoes or Potato pieces

Small Whole Onions or ½-inch slices

Whole Asparagus Spears

10-15 Minutes

Bell Pepper strips 1-inch

Eggplant slices ¼-inch

Zucchini or Yellow Squash slices ¾-inc

Whole Green Beans

20-30 Minutes

Corn on the Cob

BASIC RULES FOR GOOD MANNERS AT THE DINNER TABLE

Civilization has taught us to eat with a fork, but even now if nobody is around, we use our fingers. — Will Rogers

The Napkin

As soon as you are seated, put your napkin in your lap. If you are at a formal dinner, wait for the hostess to place hers on her lap first.

When the meal is finished put your napkin at the side of your plate. Do not crumple or refold your napkin – leave it on the table in loose folds.

Which Silverware To Use

Start at the left of your plate and work your way toward the plate with each course.

You should wait until everyone has been served before you start to eat.

When you have finished the main course, place the knife and fork beside each other on the dinner plate diagonally from the upper left to lower right, with the handles extending slightly over the plate.

Beverage

Before you take a drink, blot your lips to help keep your beverage free of food particles.

Never leave your spoon in the coffee cup.

Soup

When eating soup that is served in a bowl or soup dish, dip the soup spoon away from you, not toward you. If soup is served in a cup on a saucer, you can place the spoon on the plate and drink as you would a beverage.

Please Pass

It is okay to reach for anything at the table unless you have to stretch across your neighbor, or lean too far across the table. When something is out of reach ask the person nearest to the item to pass it to you.

Dessert

If dessert is served in a small deep bowl on another plate, place the dessert spoon on the plate when you are finished. If the bowl is shallow and wide the spoon may be left in it.

MEALTIME DON'TS

- DON'T talk with your mouth full of food.

- DON'T take too large mouthfuls of any food.

- DON'T put a beverage into your mouth if it is filled with food

- DON'T cut up your entire meal before you start to eat.Don't wave your fork or spoon around during conversation.

- DON'T encircle the plate with your arm while eating.

- DON'T wipe off silverware in a restaurant. Ask for new ones.

- DON'T push your plate back when you are finished. Let it remain until your server removes it.

- DON'T Slurp.

- DON'T blow your nose at the dinner table.

- ALWAYS eat with your mouth closed.

Index

210

W

Y, Z

NOTES

NOTES

NOTES

NOTES

NOTES

NOTES

Please send _____ copies of_____

@ _____ (U.S.) each $_____

Postage and handling @ $3.50 each $_____

TOTAL $_____

Check or Credit Card (Canada-credit card only)

Charge to my ☐ Master Card or Visa Card

account # _____

expiration date _____

signature _____

MAIL TO:
Creative Ideas Publishing
7916 N.W. 23rd St.
P.M.B. 115
Bethany, OK 73008-5135
1-800-673-0768
www.busywomanscookbook.com

Name _____

Address _____

City _____ State _____ Zip _____

Phone (day) _____ (night) _____

ORDER ON THE WEB: www.busywomanscookbook.com

— —

Please send _____ copies of
Just Enough for Two Cookbook

@ $18.95 (U.S.) each $_____

Postage and handling @ $3.50 each $_____

TOTAL $_____

Check or Credit Card (Canada-credit card only)

Charge to my ☐ Master Card or Visa Card

account # _____

expiration date _____

signature _____

MAIL TO:
Creative Ideas Publishing
7916 N.W. 23rd St.
P.M.B. 115
Bethany, OK 73008-5135
1-800-673-0768
www.busywomanscookbook.com

Name _____

Address _____

City _____ State _____ Zip _____

Phone (day) _____ (night) _____

ORDER ON THE WEB: www.busywomanscookbook.com

Please send _____ copies of_____

@ _____ (U.S.) each $_____

Postage and handling @ $3.50 each $_____

TOTAL $_____

Check or Credit Card (Canada-credit card only)

Charge to my ☐ Master Card or Visa Card

account # _____

expiration date _____

signature _____

<table>
<tr><td>

MAIL TO:
Creative Ideas Publishing
7916 N.W. 23rd St.
P.M.B. 115
Bethany, OK 73008-5135
1-800-673-0768
www.busywomanscookbook.com

</td></tr>
</table>

Name _____

Address _____

City _____ State _____ Zip _____

Phone (day) _____ (night) _____

ORDER ON THE WEB: www.busywomanscookbook.com

— —

Please send _____ copies of
Just Enough for Two Cookbook

@ $18.95 (U.S.) each $_____

Postage and handling @ $3.50 each $_____

TOTAL $_____

Check or Credit Card (Canada-credit card only)

Charge to my ☐ Master Card or Visa Card

account # _____

expiration date _____

signature _____

<table>
<tr><td>

MAIL TO:
Creative Ideas Publishing
7916 N.W. 23rd St.
P.M.B. 115
Bethany, OK 73008-5135
1-800-673-0768
www.busywomanscookbook.com

</td></tr>
</table>

Name _____

Address _____

City _____ State _____ Zip _____

Phone (day) _____ (night) _____

ORDER ON THE WEB: www.busywomanscookbook.com

SHARE YOUR FAVORITE RECIPE

Do you have a favorite quick and easy recipe? Do family and friends ask you for it? Would you like to see it in a national cookbook?

If so, please send your favorite quick and easy recipe to us. If we use it in a future cookbook, you will be given credit in the book for the recipe, and will receive a free copy of the book.

Submit to: Creative Ideas Publishing
               PMB 115
               7916 N.W. 23rd Street
               Bethany, OK 73008-5135

Special thanks to Ann Glass for sharing some of her favorite recipes.